# The Test

Jean Baréma

# The Test

*Living in the Shadow of
Huntington's Disease*

FRANKLIN
SQUARE
PRESS

New York

Published by Franklin Square Press, a division of Harper's Magazine.
666 Broadway, New York, N.Y. 10012

First English-language edition

First printing 2005

Library of Congress Cataloging-in-Publication Data

Baréma, Jean.
  [Test English]
  The test : living in the shadow of Huntington's disease / Jean Baréma.
      p.   cm.
  ISBN 1-879957-57-4 (alk. paper)
    1. Baréma, Jean—Health. 2. Huntington's chorea—France—Biography.
  3. Huntington's chorea—Diagnosis—Psychological aspects. 4. Human
  chromosome abnormalities—Diagnosis—Psychological aspects. I. Title.
  RC394.H85B37 2005
  362.196'851'0092—dc22              2005013674

Designed by Laura Lindgren

Manufactured in the United States of America

10  9  8  7  6  5  4  3  2  1

For my mother,

My older brother,

My younger sister,

For Mary, whose name is not Mary,

For our children,

For Alexandra, Marcella, Valérie.

To Woody Guthrie and Alain Souchon.

"Anxiety is the dizziness of freedom."
Søren Kierkegaard


"To know about our future or our children's future,
we don't ask the gods anymore; we ask the genes."
François Jacob,
Nobel Prize for Medicine, 1965

*Thursday, April 4: D-Day*

*Why did I come an hour early? How naive! As if hurrying could change anything about the verdict.*

*I'm sitting on a bench facing the first building you see after coming in through the stone gate, a chapel—massive, cold, dirty. Sinister, like the death sentence I'm sure to be getting an hour from now. Death, real death, with no recourse, no appeal, slow and horrible like a halting march down into degeneration and madness. Like my mother before me, whose mindless screams still haunt me twenty years later. Like my brother, who grows worse by the day, less and less capable of walking; his words slur and stumble over one another, barely forming sentences. Like my younger sister, who is beginning her own downward journey. Soon the two of them will start that screaming.*

*And maybe like me, too, depending on the luck of the genetic draw. I am about to find out what's in store for me—and for my children, and their children, all links in this infinitely tragic chain.*

*The chapel bells are ringing. Nine o'clock. Barbara must already be in her office in the Neurology/Genetics building, next door to where they treat the crazy people. She came by the elevated metro station that overlooks this hodgepodge of nineteenth-century buildings and glass-walled modern structures called a hospital, this place where thousands of people come and go between hope and despair, between the busy sounds of life and the silence of death. She walked past those hedges enclosing beds of red and yellow roses. On this spring day, they're bursting with health. The lucky things!*

*Barbara knows. Yes, the doctor knows the results of the test. Why isn't she rushing out to me, file in hand, yelling, "You haven't got it!" We would fall into each other's arms. I might kiss her. I would be happy. I would live—or anyhow, I would get to die of something else. Maybe a nice little raging cancer? Better yet, sudden death in a car accident, quick and painless.*

*Why isn't she running to me as fast as she can? It must be that she's wondering how to break the news. That's it. That's the truth. She's lingering in her office with the urine-colored walls, she's rehearsing her lines: "You're done for," she'll tell me. "So sorry." She'll probably take my hands, tenderly. But she'll say the thing bluntly. Barbara is like that. She has to be. Tender bluntness. Otherwise, how could she bear what she does? She tests people, and when the test comes out positive she has to tell them they are going to die a slow, torturous death.*

*On my bench, I shiver.*

I've known Barbara for five years now. Back on that first day, I didn't realize how beautiful she was. At that point, I wasn't noticing anything. The day was warm, a brilliant, warm day for loving life, both past and future. I, on the other hand, was groggy. I'd been alone for a whole week. Wife and children and their happy laughter gone off for vacation to the other side of the world. I was alone in Paris. Free.

Free to mope about, and then the doubt and questioning sneaked up and overwhelmed me. What if I, too... like Mother? Mother. My poor dear mother.

I was remembering: It had started with an ordinary depression, the kind familiar to all those millions of French people stuffing down antidepressants and managing, somehow, to stagger through their sad lives. For her, it was different. It was the first step toward the final knockout.

She was sitting on her bed one day in my grandparents' house when she had a sudden revelation. She was knitting. Attempting to knit, that is.

"Even this! I can't do this anymore!" she blurted in a flash of lucidity, with a tired smile on her defeated face.

Why, on that particular summer weekend morning in Paris, did I recall that moment out of the dozens of more frightening ones? Perhaps because the warm summer air reminded me of vacations at my grandparents' house by the sea. An old family house filled with large Normandy armoires. The smell of wax, and creaking floorboards that always scared us kids at night. A delicious scare, intense...alive.

But this memory, the knitting thing—a memory of living, of a realm of life, as they say, that also heralded death. No. Worse than death: the inability to live. "I can't do this anymore," she whispered again, collapsing exhausted on her bed. On the wall above her hung a little crucifix.

Paris was deserted that summer weekend and all I could think about was my mother's words, how she looked at the brink of surrender, of sinking into the world of madness and death. Only much later would I learn the name of Mother's torturer, her murderer: it was Huntington's disease.

George Summer Huntington was born in 1850 on Long Island. His father and grandfather were doctors, too. Their stories haunted George. He remembered going one day with his father, George Sr., on a house call in the countryside. Even the horse was scared. "There, before us, stood two tall, emaciated women who looked like cadavers. They were writhing in all directions, and their faces were misshapen by their contorted expressions. I was startled and frightened. What did this mean? Where could these strange creatures have come from?" In 1872, Huntington writes a report based on his father's and grandfather's observations and on his own research. For the first time, he speaks about a "hereditary chorea." *Chorea,* a Greek word, means "the dance," but St. Vitus' dance, the dance of lunatics. He describes a slow, inexorable degeneration of the central nervous system caused by a defective gene. It is transmitted from one generation to the next. The onset of the disease appears anytime between the ages of thirty-five and seventy, manifesting as depression and uncontrollable movements of the limbs, and slowly evolving toward dementia and, finally, death, within the space of five to ten years.

Huntington does not know how the gene is transmitted. He simply notes that some offspring inherit the disease and others do not. He also remarks that the disease has no name even for those who have it, or for their families, observed over three generations. They never speak about it. They just allude to "problems."

Dr. Huntington's report was to have a certain impact, particularly as it foreshadowed Mendel's discoveries about genes and heredity thirty years later.

Scientists begin to dissect the brains of some patients. One doctor compares them to "rotten cantaloupes." Genealogists get interested. They find 962 people with Huntington's disease in the New England area, with common ancestors from among four different families from England who settled in Boston and Salem, Massachusetts, during the seventeenth century. Salem...the witches of Salem, burned or hanged? Yes, them! Huntington's disease. The devil's disease!

"What if I...like the witches...like Mother...? Fifty-fifty odds of getting it?" That particular weekend, eighteen years after my mother's death, fear suddenly coursed through me, jolting me awake. This sadness weighing me down, nothing to do with any gentle melancholy. Quick—get information! I had vaguely heard of a genetic test that could predict if a person would get Huntington's. I hadn't paid much attention at the time—what good would it do to know? But now, terror. I must know. Then commit suicide before the disintegration. Or perhaps live, more and better, waiting for the stroke of the gong? What's death, after all? Einstein said it meant meeting up with Mozart in heaven. Someone else talked about seeing the Virgin Mary, the most beautiful woman of all, with her gypsy veil. Death? So what? It happens to everybody. The only difference is that I would know how—bit by bit—and approximately when.

So, a very dark Saturday. Horrible hours, no longer thinking straight, the mind carried away, hijacked by an anxiety attack. Have to know, or rather confirm, that it's all over. Phone the hospital— they have a special department, it's where my brother found out. I don't dare call him. What could he say to me anyway? His doctor told me privately that he was already mixing up reality and imagination. In any case, I'd probably reach his wife, who would again call me a murderer for not having warned her that this man she loved, my big brother, carried death inside him. She might even whisper to me what she was really thinking—that she hates him now, the way you can hate a dog turned rabid, a pet that becomes an ugly, deranged beast that you want to give a beating. Or an injection. Poor woman! What else could she possibly think or say to me? How can love and life survive this collision—head-on, slow-motion, pervasive but endless—with... death?

On Sunday I called the hospital and got an answering machine. Even Death goes away for the weekend. What should I do? There's an association for the sick and their families. It is in the suburbs. I imagine them there in their little stone house, sitting around a table covered in cheap oilcloth, in a state of shock. Some rebellious, some resigned, others discussing an article from a medical journal, reprinted in *Le Monde,* reporting brain-cell transplants... Hope. Hope for future generations. Meanwhile, the present is murky.

Yes, the house is stone. I ring the doorbell. An old lady limps to the outside gate, but she does not open it.

"What do you want?"

"Uh, is this the Huntington's Society?"

"They moved. Somewhere in the 13th arrondissement in Paris. Do you want the address?"

"Please."

She looks me over. Her face is rutted but calm, her gaze impenetrable. She must have been a doctor.

"Do you think I've got it? The disease?" The question just popped out like a shot from a gun.

"How would I know?"

"You were looking at me. As though..."

"I wasn't looking at you. Let me get the address."

It is too late for me to go to the association. And anyway, what could the members do for me? The truth is only to be found at the hospital. A blood sample. A simple blood sample, like for cholesterol. Tomorrow. But I'll have to get through the night. Why do I feel so feverish? It is a beautiful afternoon. It is warm. I don't have the flu, but I feel as though I have a fever. I stretch my arms out in front of me. Why are my hands trembling? No, they're not trembling. My mother... how was she before she fell ill? How old was she when there was the incident with her knitting? Fifty-three years old. I am forty-eight. My hour has not yet come. I'm just being dramatic. But how did she feel before that? Before Huntington's? She didn't know anything about this illness, this threat that was to befall her. Her father with his beautiful mustache died a good death at age seventy-five. Her mother, though— no way to know. A stroke had rendered her fairly helpless at the age of forty-two. And the mother's father had been a bit deranged. But nothing was more commonplace at the beginning of the twentieth century in Brittany, in that kingdom of alcoholics and intermarriage.

I know the enemy, and I know how it will attack. Quietly, slyly at first. It makes trouble for a few neurons. Nothing awful. Easy to mistake it for simple aging, everybody's enemy.

But Huntington's has its own refined ways. It is a real terrorist specializing in the slow poisoning, the time bomb ticking away that will inevitably explode. You're born with the fuse, and you live with it for years, without knowing that it's slowly burning down.

But Mother... Before the knitting incident, there was her depression. I had no idea. I was away in California at the university, discovering journalism, the real thing: politics, good guys and bad guys, writers, sitcoms, friendships, life. Mary, so beautiful, so "New World," so full of tender promises. Love. Yes, there were a few letters from my father that spoke about my mother, just vague allusions. Poor man. He never knew or dared express any weakness, nor could he share any of his fears. Never in his life. There were also a few notes from my mother, halting messages with contorted words. She mentioned her migraines, said she missed me, worried about little details. But how could I know, even when her notes came less often in more and more jagged handwriting? When I returned to France in July, my father picked me up at the airport and we drove directly to the rest home in a western suburb of Paris. Ever since, I have hated the month of July.

I see it still: the garden is pretty, perfumed and colorful. She arrives, held up by two nurses, scuffing her feet on the pebbly path. She looks gray. Everything looks gray, from her slippers to her dress. Her hair. Her skin. I give a kiss to this gray silhouette. She says nothing, shows no expression, seems to see nothing.

"It's Jean here to see you. He's back from Los Angeles. He passed all his exams. He is going to be a journalist."

She knows that's always been my dream, ever since I was a child and learned to read via newspapers. But still she says nothing, shows no sign of life in her eyes, sees nothing. The nurse is quick to inform me that my mother is groggy from the anxiety medication, that she has just come out of sleep therapy. I glance over at my father, a not-too-tall man with rounded shoulders. He straightens up as though to better face up to the unmentionable, the incomprehensible. *Why is she so unhappy?* he is wondering. He feels guilty. But of what? His eyes are glistening. The nurses take away the gray shape. In the car, I cry.

That evening my father and I dine together. We talk a little. Not much. I try to revive my mother. Happy memories: the ocean, which I feared, even in her arms; the picnics, the soccer matches; the things of life. He asks me about my diploma, about what I will be doing, about Mary. My future, so as to make the present vanish. He was probably right to do so.

A few days later, Mother changed hospitals. They lowered the narcoleptic doses. My father took her to a place in the provinces. He came back a few days later, still with tears in his eyes.

"She told me she wants to die."

She would die, but not until five years later. Of what? I was not to know. The death warrant said a heart attack. Too much medication, too much terror within, too far within. Before that, she must have lived through an infinity of hours, of minutes, of seconds. She would be moved from the bed to the chair, then from the chair to the bed, then from one bed to another bed. At first at home, then at the hospital—actually, at the asylum.

I would go see her, singing this children's song to myself:

> *C'est aujourd'hui dimanche,*
> *...et ma jolie maman...*
> *Là, là...des roses blanches.*

I had to park the car and climb a long paved pathway. It was
always raining. People walked around the grounds, crazy people.
Some of them make gargoyle eyes at you. Sometimes a woman—it
was always the same one—would squat froglike on the path and
defecate, laughing the laugh of a damned person. My mother was in
a large room with three other patients. There was absolute silence,
which she would break from time to time. She didn't move, but a
cry would come from deep in her throat. Her mouth was barely
open, but she would cry out, exhaling some overflow of terror or
using up her last shreds of life. One day an ambulance brought her
to my parents' home in the country. She was escorted to the garden,
never uttered a word, and then went back to the asylum. There she
smiled at a nurse and tried to speak a word, I was told later. "Rose,"
she whispered. She had seen roses in her garden, and this was her
first word in five years. The next day, she was dead.

On Monday at dawn I fell apart. The night before, in her little stone
house, the old lady who was perhaps a doctor had not been reassuring. I hadn't managed to reach anyone. I hadn't slept all night. I
had only one thing in mind—that in the morning I would call the
hospital. I would take the test. If I didn't have the gene, I'd go out
and get drunk. Otherwise . . . well, I'd worked up a lot of plans: I
could throw myself off the sixth floor of our apartment building.
Banal. Or I could join my family in the wooded hills of Massachusetts—there's a bridge over a gorge there, about two hundred yards
high with white rapids running below, and I could jump. Romantic.
Or else go to the Grand Canyon, the most beautiful place in the
whole wide world. I could run, take the challenge and leap into this
split earth, this bottomless abyss. Metaphysical.

I got out of bed like a rooster with its head cut off. Walking unsteadily, I went to my office at the newspaper. I ran the daily editorial meeting, barely containing my snickers at the sight of these future cadavers babbling around the table. I could only think about death while what's-his-name over there, that ectoplasm, that bundle of frustrations in the shape of a man, that fake journalist, fake man, false friend, kept talking solemnly about his evening with some stupid silicon starlet, and we absolutely HAD to publish his great scoop— that she was now thinking about doing "cinemaaaaaaa." Imbecile, too stupid to realize that he's just a lousy mercenary for a mediocre sheet serving up pabulum to the puppets pretending to be actors while they waited to die.

Then I shut myself up in my office. I called the neurology department where my brother was being treated. A friendly nurse answered.

"My mother died eighteen years ago of Huntington's disease my brother has it now and I'm afraid I have it," I spewed out all in one breath.

She didn't say anything.

"I want to take the test. I know there is one. I want to do it today."

"Very well, but it won't be possible today."

"Okay, well, tomorrow then."

"No, you can't do it either today or tomorrow."

She explained that one could only take the test after a long process involving discussions with genetic counselors, neurologists, and psychiatrists who specialized in Huntington's. This drama required preparation. It would be long and slow and drawn out. She told me her first name was Isabelle. I was expecting something worse, like Ethel or Hazel or a prison warden's name; she had the name of a queen.

Lunchtime. A meeting with my oldest friend, a man I have gone off with in the past to cover big, magnificent stories for our newspaper, reports full of great wars in faraway lands. Serge was waiting in a bistro at the Place des Ternes. He always had the same smile, warm but tired, of a faithful old friend. The day my mother died, I was supposed to go to Israel on a story. I called him and he immediately agreed to replace me, with his legendary enthusiasm, his zest for going everywhere to tell about life as it is, the only story that matters. His talent and enthusiasm had cost him his marriage. His wife didn't know the only rule worth following—à la Paulo Coelho: "Today is the first day of the rest of your life." Serge knows it. He follows it with an intensity that excludes neither perspective nor wisdom.

By the middle of lunch, I had hardly said a thing.

"What's wrong?" he murmured.

I burst into sobs. "I think I'm sick with the same thing my mother died of: Huntington's. Take me to the hospital."

We took a taxi. I gave Serge the name of the hospital, my wife's phone number in the States, my older sister's phone number on vacation, and the name of Isabelle, the nurse. What a strange moment. As we passed the Arc de Triomphe, despite my complete panic I nonetheless had time to think consciously and coolly that it was the last time I'd ever see it. What can I say—it was almost exciting.

Isabelle was expecting me. She is used to desperate people.

"You called this morning, didn't you?"

"Yes."

"Sit down. I'll go find someone for you."

I sat in an armchair with Serge beside me. There must have been other people there because I stopped crying. I was afraid to appear ridiculous. Isabelle returned with someone.

"This is Barbara. She is a neurologist. You should talk to her."

I talked to Barbara. Two and a half hours. About my mother, my brother, my anxiety, and my depression. "Isn't this how it all begins?"

"Twelve million French people are depressed," she told me. "For the moment, you're just one among them. I've been observing you these past few minutes, and I don't see any sign at all of Huntington's. At least, not for the moment."

Barbara gave me a Xanax, and a prescription so that I could take two more in the evening. She also gave me an appointment for the next day. Serge took me home. I went to bed. I slept for fourteen hours. When I woke up, it was a gorgeous day and I no longer thought I was about to die. Medication is such a miracle! I was even in a good mood, so much so that I considered going to a funny movie and laughing. Yesterday I was a wreck, and today I was going back to see Barbara like a gentleman calling on a lady. Actually, what did she look like? I didn't remember.

She was beautiful. She is beautiful. Especially her eyes. That is the only thing that matters, isn't it? The only thing that's alive.

My brother does not show much life anymore. I took him to lunch the other day. He can hardly walk, as though each part of his body is separate from the other: the foot, the ankle, the knee, the hip, the hand, the wrist, the elbow, the shoulder, the neck. Each part works on its own, each against the other. People look at him in the street. Some of them laugh. Idiots! But if they looked him in the eyes . . . well, those are alive still, a little. He hardly talks now. His words get lost in his lower jaw, which sags as though it weighs too much. It's his misery that weighs too much. But his eyes are alive, and they brighten when we speak of a happy memory.

"Do you remember, Big Brother. . ." I was thirteen, he was fifteen. There were these girls at the Parc de St. Cloud. They were wearing dark blue pleated skirts and kneesocks the same color. We followed them, at first from afar, hiding behind trees. They saw us, laughed us off, and quickened their pace. They hid and jumped out at us from behind a bush. We tried to catch them, but they escaped and ran away laughing. We never saw them again. "Do you remember that?"

His eyes searched and remembered; he laughed. And then cried. Life had gone by, was going on without him.

Barbara has beautiful eyes. Brown. Round. Huge. She speaks as though she knows me through and through. Her brown hair, sun bur-nished with red highlights, falls on her forehead and face to round out her angular features. She talks to me, about me. Did I tell her so much yesterday when I was crying? She understands about my anxieties. She separates out the commonplace—the exhilarating but exhausting career, family, twenty-five years of marriage, three grown children—from the real anxiety, the real and only one, this black pit that is a death foretold: Huntington's . . .

"Am I sick?"

A little smile crosses her lips, she shrugs her shoulders, turns her palms upward (I notice she has pianist's fingers). She says, "How should I know?"

"But—my anxiety attacks, my feverishness, my muscle aches; it must be Huntington's!"

"Did you come by car?"

"Why do you ask?"

"Where did you park?"

"In front of the hospital. What does it matter to you?"

"It doesn't, but a person with Huntington's often loses his short-term memory. You're not there yet."

"Are you trying to reassure me?"

"No, I can't reassure you, but you have no reason to worry either. Maybe you do carry the gene. Your mother died of the disease. Your brother has it. You are in a group that is 'at risk.' There's a 50 percent chance you'll get it. But for the moment, life goes on. I'm going to give you some antidepressants. A few million French people are taking them. Most of them will die of the usual causes. Stop worrying."

She gets up, holds out her hand to shake mine and looks at me. She is as tall as I am. Her smile and eyes are compassionate. Pleasant. She gives me a prescription.

"It will take at least fifteen days before these drugs start to work. In the meantime, if you have an anxiety attack, take one or two Xanax. I'll see you in a month. We'll talk about the test again."

"Am I sick?"

"For the moment, you're like everyone else—you are mortal. Just mortal."

"I'm sure you know without having to do the test."

"Yes, for some people, I can tell just by looking at them and listening to them. For you, no. Goodbye. You are condemned to live. Like everybody."

I leave the hospital. I look at "everybody." Future cadavers, every last one. No exceptions. Which of us will die first? That bum over there, lying on the pavement, dead-drunk? Or this stressed-out man rushing across the street? Or that young woman on the bench reading a book? Or me? I decide to walk home rather than take the metro. I think about Woody Allen, who starts philosophizing when he is feeling serious and hypochondriacal. In the film *Manhattan*, Mariel Hemingway has just left him. He is lying on his couch. He wants to die. Right away. But first he thinks of all the things that could keep him here—Mariel's sad smile, a Knicks game at Madison Square Garden, a Chopin nocturne. He sighs and decides to postpone his departure from this world. I sigh. Why not kill myself right now?

What is holding me back? My wife? She is far away. Does she really love me anyway? Enough. Twenty-five years of marriage can wear you out. A lot of times I seem to get on her nerves. "You are so antisocial," she'll say. And I'll reply, "Yes, but that's part of my charm. You can't love everybody." "All you ever think about is soccer," she'll say, irritated. And I reply, "Yeah, well, a soccer match is a life." What could be more exciting? She'll finish by saying, "You never take me in your arms anymore." I'm not sure how to respond to that. Once I dared to say, "Do you really want me to?" She nearly slapped me.

The memory makes me smile. I feel like talking to her, just to see. But what will I say? That I just left the hospital? That I'm coming out of a bout of terror set off by this bitch Huntington's? Have we ever talked in depth about this time bomb of a disease? No, of course not. We didn't really know. We didn't know the risks involved. Actually, we didn't WANT to know. So we went ahead and had three children. As though there was no issue. Telling ourselves that by the time they were adults, there'd be a cure. Dream on! But now, do we have to stop living and give up everything? One-to-two odds I had Huntington's. Two-to-two we die anyhow. So why not bet on living?

I go home. Two messages on the answering machine. Serge wants to know how I'm doing. Just listening to his voice has a calming effect. He invites me to dinner tomorrow. Dear Serge! He'd never let me down. The other message is from Mary in Massachusetts. She says she tried to reach me at the office. My secretary told her I was home with the flu. She asks me how I am, tells me about the weather there. Magnificent. The kids have gone swimming. Magnificent. She tells me she loves me, that she misses me.

I call her back and tell her nothing. At least, not what happened these past forty-eight hours. What good would it do? Life goes on, Barbara said. Okay, so let life go on.

I go to bed. Suddenly, the anxiety is back. That empty hole, immense, endless, with no edges and no words. I clutch my sheets. I am sweating, I'm cold. I'm afraid, the worst kind of fear, the kind you can't do anything about because it takes in everything and drowns everything. It is strange and a pity that it has no opposite on the happiness scale. Maybe orgasm? But that is so fleeting, ungraspable, brief. God? Where is that God of peace and serenity? In Xanax.

The doctor explained that depression is very simple: the brain doesn't produce enough serotonin, so the tranquilizers and antidepressants restore the balance. I grab my little white bottle with the violet spot. Two pills. I already feel better. I become sensible again. I close the shutters, because I live on the sixth floor and I am afraid some impulse might seize me during an anxiety attack. I fall asleep, I then wake with a jolt. I dreamed about a storm. The tip of the lightening bolt struck me on my forehead. I'm standing up in my bed. Exhausted. I'm not thinking about my mother or my brother anymore, only about myself. What's happening to me, the person people say is so rational, almost too rational? Am I sick because I'm stressed or am I stressed because I'm sick? According to Barbara, children of people with Huntington's spend a lot of their time watching for the symptoms even though they don't carry the gene. I think about her again. She has a long face with strong cheekbones. Her eyes are soft and tender—maybe she's nearsighted—and her voice has a slight accent.

She must be of foreign origin. I wonder what she's like when she makes love. Why am I thinking this? I laugh. I'm afraid. Someone once told me that one symptom of Huntington's is the loss of inhibitions. I take another Xanax. I fall asleep.


A few days later, I leave for the United States, Massachusetts. Vacation, my wife, the kids. In the plane, I wonder what I'm going to tell Mary. And when? She is waiting for me at Logan airport in Boston. She looks gorgeous. People are happy. It is sunny. How can a person be sick? I took two Xanax before landing. Huntington's?—what's Huntington's? The New England mountains look like paradise. The shingled house reminds me of Disney movies, so perfect and homey. We make love. Her skin is warm; her breasts are nice and round. A few drops of sweat lie on her high forehead. Her body arches. We moan with pleasure. Oh, God, what happened to me in Paris? We'll see tomorrow.

The next day we go to a party. A few minutes before we get there, I stop the car. There is no one on the road. We can smell freshly cut grass. A river is running nearby.

"I fell apart in Paris."

"I know."

"What? What do you mean? How did you know?"

"I called your office and they told me you had the flu. You're never sick, and the flu in the middle of July? And it's not like you to stay in bed even if you *are* sick."

We never got to the party. The birds were chirping, the water was gurgling in the river, the leaves of the trees were whispering. I talked to Mary for an hour about what happened.

"My mother—you remember my mother. You always thought she was a little weird. You know, her arm movements, those twisted grins that weren't exactly smiles, her nervousness about minor things, the migraines she tried to dismiss. The doctors she'd see who wouldn't tell her anything. Because they didn't know anything! She loved me; people say I was her favorite. When she was young, she looked like Michèle Morgan in *Le Quai des Brumes*. At fifty she was more like Simone Signoret in *La Veuve Couderc*. Do you remember when she died, twenty years ago, during the summer in Brittany? You were in the States and I phoned you. With no particular feeling or emotion. To tell the truth, I was relieved. So was my father. So were my brothers and sisters. We had never spoken about it among ourselves. But all I could think of was euthanasia. What was the point of her life in that hospital bed, silent except for her screaming, those empty eyes, already dead? She had to be fed, held up to walk, washed because she soiled herself. But when the nurse told me the story of the roses and I saw her dead, finally dead after all that suffering, I cried. I really cried. What a blinding mystery. One minute you're looking at a living cadaver wishing her the relief of death...and then you see her dead and finally calm and serene—the pain is unbearable. A person never gets over the death of his mother, even if it's a deliverance. At the church service, I cried again. For the condolences, I got into the line ahead of my father. I don't know why. And I was still crying. I wanted to be first so I could silently scream out, 'She's alive!' 'Down with death!' I wanted to scream that this bitch of a gene with its programmed death couldn't do anything anymore to my mother. She'd lived for fifty-eight years. She had beautiful children. She had loved, she had suffered, and she had possibly given us this *fucking Huntington's gene*. Meanwhile, she had lived. Do you remember, Mary, I told you all this? You'd come back to France, and we were leaving the cemetery, both happy and sad. Like life. We talked about us. For some strange reason, you told me then that you had cheated on me once. One evening on a transatlantic ship, one crazy, alcohol-filled evening. For some reason, it struck me as natural. I mean, that you cheated on me and that you told me at that moment. Death makes life even more so. A few weeks later, we started our first child. And then we made a second one and then a third. And we went on living. Happily. With passion for life despite the risks. Because you have to live, and defy the bitch... until the day you go down."

A deer came to drink at the river's edge. I kept on talking about the gaping darkness, the fear that catches up with you. My lunch with Serge. My encounter with Barbara at the hospital.

"Did you take the test?" Mary asked the question abruptly as though to do away with the most haunting Damocles' sword invented by nature or God to terrify mankind.

"No. The uncertainty gives me hope. If I take the test and it's positive, I'll kill myself. I'd rather not know."

We went back to our cozy wooden house. In the following weeks, we played golf, we toured New England. I stopped taking the anti-depressants. When we went back to France, I saw Barbara and told her I had stopped taking them. I felt calm now, I told her. I was keeping the beast at bay. I was getting used to it.

What an idiot! A few days later, at the office, I have the umpteenth blowup with the boss. He never knows what he wants. Damn! Absolute when he says white, absolute when he says black. Unbearable! I accuse him of being intellectually inconsistent—the ultimate insult for a man full of complexes, who can only think in figures, who gets his culture at specified hours—tonight it's Wagner with spaghetti!—and when one of his employees commits suicide, he tells his PR man that the man probably had AIDS so what do you expect?

He's going to fire me. He doesn't like provocation and I've always been provocative. That's another symptom. I am afraid. With Huntington's, you get irritable, and this boss irritates me! Like what's-her-name before him, at another magazine where I worked. She paid a lot to get rid of me. I'm scared. It's going to start again, I can tell. I break down. I cry. Over my mother, my brother. Over me, especially. I'm going to end up like them. I phone Barbara. She tells me to come to the hospital. I know the way so perfectly. It runs in front of the Crazy House, the three low buildings where, in the nineteenth century, six hundred patients were kept in tiny rooms; outside, half-moon benches were anchored to the stone wall. Some are still there. The patients used to be chained to them on the rare occasions when they were allowed out to get some fresh air.

In the hallway in front of Barbara's office, a madwoman is waiting. You could almost say she is my mother. She is gray like her, skin and bones like her, in a daze like her. Had she been beautiful like my mother? Happy, like my mother? Probably, but so what? Her head drops to her chest suddenly, as though her muscles have given up. And just as suddenly, she raises her head. An arm starts gesticulating, hitting the air, a twisted wrist, three fingers spread out and the other two folded in. It looks as if a puppeteer on the ceiling is manipulating her body wildly. I feel I'm seeing myself a few months down the road. I want to talk to her. "Don't be afraid, madame," I say dopily, as though I were comforting myself. She looks at me. Half of her mouth opens. Is she trying to smile? Nothing. Her mouth closes.

"Are you crying?" Barbara stands before me. I feel stupid with tears in my eyes—me, the professional cynic who has covered wars and death the world over, led teams of journalists, harangued big shots at dinner parties, dined at the best restaurants, slept in the finest hotels. And here I am whining in this nondescript office. It's brand-new and it's already old, the table is made of Formica, the

floor is worn linoleum tile. And a woman in a white smock is asking me if I am crying?

"Just tell me I'm sick!"

"You are not sick. Not yet, anyhow."

"Then why am I so anxious, depressed, desperate, if I don't have
Huntington's?"

"Because you have every reason to feel that way: your mother's
death, your brother's illness, work-related stress, and being a fifty-
year-old man. And you're wondering about this terrible disease and
whether the gene is in you or not. These are all valid reasons for
feeling the way you do."

"What if I took the test?"

"It's up to you."

"What do others like me decide?"

"Well, generally, they don't take the test. They're afraid because
they know there is no remedy. But the ones who do take the test
and find out they have the gene don't commit suicide, either. In
fact . . . how can I say? They live differently. Maybe better, because
they know what to expect. They may take advantage of the good
days while they can. In fact, it's strange—people who find out they
don't have the gene sometimes react less well. They feel guilty
about their brothers or sisters who might have it. And suddenly,
there's a void facing them. Can you imagine? All at once, they know
nothing about their future. Whether you like it or not, the fear of
Huntington's gives a structure to one's life. It's a useful pivot point.
Do you know the Chinese proverb—'You only live twice. The first
time is when you are born; the second time is when you are facing
death.'"

"Yes, but why do I keep crying?"

"Because you aren't taking your medication. And so that I'll take
you seriously. Actually, you aren't crying anymore."

It was true. I laughed out loud. So did she. I left her office. The sick lady, the truly sick one, was still waiting in the hall. I leaned over and gave her a hug. She managed a half smile. Life goes on.

I sent Barbara flowers with a little note. I wrote that I always arrived at her office feeling panicky and always left feeling calm and peaceful, which in view of the circumstances was no small feat. I thanked her for her devotion and congratulated her for being who she was.

I wondered if people always fall in love with their doctor. But this I kept to myself.

At Roland-Garros stadium, the French Tennis Open. I spend my days there ever since my boss fired me and replaced me with my assistant. My assistant won't be provocative, at least. I even said that to my ex-boss, who wanted to see me again, probably out of remorse.

"You are right, he won't be provocative. In this place, cowardice triumphs." He wasn't joking. Me neither. Yet I should. Why do I take life so seriously? Why do I get annoyed all the time? Why do things drive me crazy? There's only one explanation: a Huntington's symptom, irritability.

Once again I fall apart. On center court, Cedric Pioline and Marat Safin are playing like boxers, but I'm the one who's knocked out. The crowd is in heaven, and all I can think about is a plastic bag. Like the one that Bernard Buffet used to suffocate himself after taking a handful of tranquilizers. Apparently, that's the best way to go without suffering too much. I think about Roger Quilliot, the former mayor of Clermont-Ferrand, a militant for the right to die with dignity. He killed himself, too, because he was sick. Luckily, I have my sunglasses on. The person next to me doesn't see the tears rolling down my face.

What is it that sets off these anxiety attacks? Life's little miseries? Or is it, as the Huntington's brochures say, the progressive cell changes in specific areas of the brain, notably the striatum, whose function is essential for executing the messages from the cortex? How can I find out? Easy. Take the test devised by some geniuses who discovered the anomaly in Huntington's patients: their chromosome number 4 (of twenty-three pairs) has a rickety gene. Its DNA molecules are out of whack. The molecules are chains made up of four chemical elements: adenine (A), thymine (T), guanine (G), and cytosine (C). They make up a code that determines what kind of protein a particular gene will make. Any change in the sequence causes a problem in the way the protein functions. In people who have Huntington's, the CAG sequence goes awry in a gene in the fourth pair of chromosomes. A normal gene has ten to thirty CAG triplets. If there are between thirty and forty triplets, there is a small risk; more than forty triplets and you're slated for the horror. Since 1993 it has become possible to measure the CAG sequence. Ever since, thousands of families at risk now live with the obsession: to know or not to know, that is the question.

Pioline has won. The crowd roars with delight and begins to leave the stadium. I snap out of it, having been thinking about another match. Played already, that one. Its outcome is registered on my genetic identity card. All it takes is a blood test. I take off my sunglasses. An old man is looking at me. I tell him I'm okay. I go home. I act as though all is well. I'm unemployed. I have a little bit of money, but I have a wife, three kids, minimum health insurance, and this nanomicron-sized bomb that may be eating away my brain.

.      .      .

"You okay?" Mary asks.

She is extraordinary, Mary. I'm jobless, I may have given my "thing" to her children, and she gives me her support. She sits down next to me. To comfort me, she says things she doesn't believe for one second. Ain't life beautiful?

"I might have something cooking at a newspaper," I answer her. "This one is a serious possibility."

I don't believe a word of it myself. For weeks now they've been making me promises. But the smart aleck who runs the newspaper is just playing around with me and the rumors of my possible arrival at the newspaper for his favorite game: destabilizing some of his pawns as he moves them around on his miserable chessboard according to his mood of the day. What use is this guy, or my other editor? What makes them happy? Don't they know that life is tragic? They have the most wonderful toys in the world, newspapers. They could be using them to entertain the crowds, tell stories, get people worked up, and stimulate our neurons. But they're just little shopkeepers. What do they think about from the time they get up in the morning until the sun sets? A nice paragraph put together by one of their employees? A story that will rock the republic? A heart-wrenching story about poor, unfortunate people? Or some story about honest folks? No, sir. These so-called journalist/editors are just experts in cunning and trickery, impotent admirers of good-looking prostitutes, geniuses at misusing a social resource for personal gain. How can we rely on people like them?

Once I tried to knock over the hurdle. It was at my other newspaper. I was in the jail keeper's office. I could sense that my end was near, that I was going to be fired. A long time earlier, he had confided that his daughter had cystic fibrosis, and that he had heart problems. The guy was human. I felt like talking about my problems, the risks I ran of winding up out in the cold. I told him about my brother, and my worry that I might end up like him. He never blinked an eye! And then, when I was fired, he was right out in front, ready for the kill.

Once again, I was a sucker. I am a terrible judge of people. But luckily he kept my secret to himself. Can you imagine if he had told everyone in the business: "Oh, you know whatchamacallit, he's got a fifty-fifty chance of becoming a vegetable within the next few years." Who would hire me? Like my banker: I applied for a loan at a time when I still had a job. There was a questionnaire: Are your parents still alive? If not, what was the cause of their death? Do you have any brothers or sisters who are ill? If yes, what is their illness? And I had to take an AIDS test. I knew that test didn't pose a problem. But why don't they also ask for a test for Huntington's? And soon, one that predicts if you are going to get cancer of the prostate, or the ovaries, or the exact date of your heart attack. Come on, for good-ness' sake, let us live! I lied to my banker, to my insurance broker, to the company doctor. Like I did to everyone.

Let me live out the rest of my life, at least!

I go to bed. Take a Xanax. I dream about a little boy with blond hair, alone in the middle of a giant chessboard. I am standing behind a rope stretched around this platform. I hold out my arm to the boy. I can't reach him. Am I the little blond boy, or is it my sick brother, already far away and out of reach? I keep trying. My arm stretches out. I grab him. We are on a road. The little boy has turned into my brother. We are running a marathon; I am ahead and he's hanging in. I cheer him on. We need to reach the finish line just a few hundred yards ahead. He can't make it. He stops and disappears from my nightmare. Now I am in a house in a run-down section of town. My teeth are falling out, one by one. I am dying. I run, I flee. A dead end, or rather two blocked streets, one by skinheads with weapons straight out of a horror film, the other by an enormous machine: huge steel pistons steadily rising and falling like huge teeth, with just a few seconds to get through them before being squashed and mangled. But beyond them is light. I choose that path. I get through the pistons. An old lady is waiting for me on the other side, a kindly witch who takes me by the hand and leads the way. My teeth keep falling out. My mouth is bloody. I feel like I'm in the Middle Ages, in heaven or in hell. Is this my mother who is leading me to troughs of dirty water mixed with blood and rotting fish? I wash my face in it.

I wake up panting. Is this a preview of what awaits me when my neurons have disintegrated enough so that I no longer qualify merely as a person at risk but as one who's sick? Why was my mother screaming that way in her bed in the mental institution? Maybe she was seeing rotting fish.

My daughter comes to get me out of bed. She wants me to take her to school. She is splendid, my daughter. Twelve years old and always in a good humor. She never knew my mother, but she knows about my brother. She has even been told that I might get sick like him. She didn't believe it, or she didn't understand. Or she doesn't want to believe it or understand it. She has probably buried it in some corner of her memory, a burning ember that will flare up again someday, or in some nightmare. Anyhow, she never spoke about it again. Unlike her seventeen-year-old brother, a genuine tortured soul, who yelled at me the other day because he felt little twinges in his legs or arms or face. I told him not to worry, that when I was his age, I would find signs of skin cancer on myself every day. I told him he had nothing to fear as long as I was not sick, and he should have only one aim, one obsession: to live and live well. *Did he believe me?* I wonder.

I take my daughter to school. I still don't have a job. What shall I do today? Call some old friends? Go back home and sleep? Kill myself? I go home to sleep. I am ashamed. I'm afraid. Going back to bed at ten o'clock in the morning is a sign of depression. And people with Huntington's are depressed, so I must have it! I go back to bed anyway, sleep until noon. My back hurts when I wake up. I hurt all over all the time. Like my brother. Another symptom.

I told this to Barbara. She made fun of me. She said that after fifty, if a person wakes up with no aches and pains he must be dead. She laughed at her joke. I like her laugh; it's hearty and all the more amazing for someone who lives daily with tragedy. Except for when she announces to someone that their test was negative, that they're on the right team. How does that go? Do you know just by looking at her when she walks out to get you from the hallway outside her office, when she's still ten yards off, when she comes up with her hand out? Does she dress differently according to the verdict she's going to render? Does she eat the same thing at breakfast that day? Does she listen to the same kind of music before taking the metro to work?

*Thursday, April 4: D-Day*

*On the bench, there in front of the chapel, I shiver. A half hour more. I should never have come. I should never have taken the blood test. Where is Barbara? What is she doing? I'm frightened. I have known her for five years. For five years, I have been coming to this hospital. I am going to phone her. I phone her. No answer. The chapel bell rings the half hour. How does a future death-row prisoner feel a half hour before the jury returns with the verdict?*

Life is beautiful. I got a job. Two, in fact. My former magazine wants me back. And a large-circulation magazine called me to head up their journalism team. I decide to take the plunge. Talk about success. Some friends will make fun of me, those who are still in the hard-news business and still believe in it. *Believe in what?* I wonder. I used to believe in it, too. It had been my dream and I did it. I took on the whole world, war zones, the back rooms of diplomacy, and the secrets of decision makers. I was useful, surely. Maybe. But for what? For wretched desertion by my company. I ran afoul of some powerful figures with a few investigative articles that made them nervous. In revenge, they worked up a whole false dossier on me, full of invented crimes, and distributed it to various publications and government agencies. Some people believed it. My company failed to back me up. I was disgusted and angry; I quit. Besides, I couldn't stand my boss anymore; we would argue over the least little thing. I'd get indignant, I'd rant and rave. I was actually scared. Huntington's again? Quick anger was a symptom—what if this was the cause of these outbursts?

But what an illusion to think that things would be calmer at a less intellectual magazine! I still erupt with violence over a badly written article, or against an aging journalist who thinks he can serve up a concoction of false values and still wants to be given special

status, or against a union foreman who makes the Communist Party
chief look like a pussycat while he commits one error after another
and hides behind union rules. I fume, I storm, and I rail against
them all. At dinner parties too: the other day we were at the home
of my wife's friend, and someone turned on the radio to catch the
results of the soccer match. Paris Saint-Germain is my team, and
they'd been skinned alive. The other guests teased me for being a
PSG fan. I got mad and attacked some of them for their go-along
politics. I was right, of course. But why do I get out of control like
that? I scare people. And I scare myself.

At the office, one of the people who thinks I persecute him
described me to a colleague who later reported that he had said I
was "red like the Soviet flag. Incredible. Worrisome, in fact. Practi-
cally pathological." But what does he know, that idiot, who's so ready
to throw me in with the crazies? A lot of people appreciate me. I can
tell. I know it. This energy propels me, this enthusiasm and the rages
that are just the other side of that coin—they're attractive to people,
at least to those people I consider genuine.

"I like the way you are," I am often told by a woman journalist I
knew at my former job. "I like the way you think," said the pretty
young girl I run into in the halls. It is strange how I am beginning
to interest women despite my fifty years, my beer belly, and my
moodiness. Strange but glorious: I suddenly feel like playing this
game of seduction. How come I've lost my inhibitions? Must be the
Huntington's. The fear of having the disease is making me appreciate
present pleasures all the more. Either that or the illness is destroying my brain, my neurons. I have to ask Barbara.

.        .        .

She laughs at my question. "I think you're ready to stop the antide-pressants."

"Are you sure it's not Huntington's? I read somewhere that you lose your inhibitions along with your neurons, that Huntington's people just sort of let go. My brother..."

"Oh, be quiet. You're getting on my nerves!"

Her warning turned my behavior from stubborn stupidity to timid schoolboy. She softened her tone.

"I'm sorry, but stop mixing up your head problems with your libido. You have a one-in-two chance of carrying the gene. Who knows? Maybe the Big Bad H *has* already started to ravage your brain. But frankly, right now you're just acting like any middle-aged man in a humdrum struggle with humdrum libido issues. By the way, you should watch your weight. Anyway, I am neither a sex expert nor a marriage counselor; I can't do anything for you there. So if you will excuse me, I have genuinely *sick* people to see. Goodbye."

So that's how she dismissed me. I was not pleased. I thought I was special, a member of an extraordinary club closed to all but those confronted with the most tragic menace known to mankind—thus, exceptional human beings—and there she was, brutally turning me back to my unexceptional condition of the faithful husband sud-denly excited by two women who show an interest. "Humdrum" was the word she used. Typical. Too typical. Because yes, the disease— or at least the *possible* disease—is distancing me, gradually, from Mary. I am only too aware that day by day it is becoming the pivot point—inevitable, ineradicable, unavoidable—of my life. Will it break us apart? Mary no longer talks to me about it, nor does she mention my brother. She never asks a single question or shows any compassion. And why should she, after all? There is no reason to get morbid or to indulge in sentimentality. Still, she must instinctively realize that as a future victim I have earned a few inalienable rights: the right to absolute cynicism, basic grumpiness, eternal permission for any whim, however childish; to flamboyant indignation, however unjustified; to erratic moods. Hard to live with? You bet! And? That's love, isn't it? In our marriage vows, didn't we say we would put up with each other for better or for worse? Yet after twenty-five years of marriage, Mary no longer grants me these rights. My rants get on her nerves, my pleasures annoy her, my weaknesses make her hostile, my wounds prove she is right: they are all due to my excesses. But how can she not understand that the Damocles' sword hanging over me and maybe already destroying my neurons is exacerbating what's deepest in me? And what probably drew her to me twenty-five years ago? Has age turned me into a cynic? Probably. But how come other people find me irritating but appealing, demanding but fair, always ranting but always constructive?

"You just want to skewer people, grind them out like a cigarette butt," she threw out once during a fight. "I've known that ever since your argument with Jim. I never should have married you!"

Jim? That's the man who introduced us. He was an American beanpole, a Quaker and a Republican, the owner of a summer camp in Spain where Mary and I were both counselors in the seventies. I remember it perfectly. Jim, a conservative who wasn't always gentlemanly, had decided that one of the counselors had to cut his long hair. I stood up to his authoritarian manner, probably overreacting but not vulgar or excessively aggressive. And now Mary brings this up from the past. I crumble. I feel like she's saying that she doesn't love me anymore. Or worse, that she never did love me. Unless I really have changed. "Me, nasty?" Sure, to idiots, I'll be nasty any day! But that's healthy, no? Or is it the disease?

I am feeling alone.

I took my brother to the PSG soccer match. The team is doing badly. Surely the players will make a comeback. Not my brother—he totters. There are only a few steps to climb. I hold on to him. He arches and sticks me with his elbow. He can't help it. Before the game, we had dinner. He loves lamb chops. With each bite he just barely misses poking out his eye. But he does not want any help—his way of saying he is still alive. He hardly speaks anymore. My father and sister do what they can for him. But it is obviously his wife who is getting destroyed. She hates all of us. Poor thing! What else can she do?

One day when I was bringing my brother back from the hospital, and the doctor had said he didn't know how long this ordeal would last, she said, right in front of him because she couldn't control herself: "What? This shitty disease is going to ruin my life for years more?" I don't think my brother really heard her or understood. In any case, his face betrayed nothing. What admirable stoicism. Or else his brain was already fogged up from the disease. But she loves him, too; I am sure of that. At the restaurant he wanted to call her, to tell her something. He couldn't manage his cell phone. I dialed the number for him. I got his wife on the phone and said my name. Before I could even add that I was putting him on, she panicked: "What's wrong? What's wrong?" There was nothing wrong; nothing but the usual stuff under the reign of Huntington's disease.

.    .    .

I wonder if I shouldn't leave my wife. We don't talk anymore. The other day we quarreled in front of the kids—we were on a ski vacation in the Alps—and I went home alone to Paris. In the train, it was crystal clear to me: we should separate. The next day she returned to Paris with the children. I hardly said hello to her. She hardly did to me either. Two days later I spoke.

"How can you dislike me so much?" I asked her.

She began to cry. So did I. She made a general remark about demons that she felt were haunting me. "Of course I know why you are a bit upset these days."

But then that was it. Nothing, not even a tender word or gesture. Why have we become so incapable of true intimacy? Maybe she can tell that I have fantasies about other women, such as the woman from my old magazine. What if I were to make love to her? She is pretty, in her own way. Sometimes she resembles one of those immigrants landing at Ellis Island early in the past century, in an American propaganda film, her hair undone, and with the lost look of a wounded woman.

One day she told me about an uncle . . . sexual advances . . . she was fourteen years old. Incurable wound. Marriage later on to an accountant. An ass. Three children. She left him. Then a wonderful artist type, a little mad. "He's the one I loved the best," she said. He beat her. She left him. Then came a tortured musician. "He kept telling me he couldn't ever love anyone. I got tired of him soon enough." And now me.

"You are the first man I've never felt the least bit of contempt for." She writes me notes, tells me she loves me. She is so desperate, basically, that she is always cheerful if you treat her with respect and sympathize with her despair. Which I do. I find her sexy. She is petite. Nice body. Eyes that have swallowed and digested all her wounds, eyes that make her sensual. I want her. Why? Because, as Barbara would say,

my fifty-year-old libido is acting up? Or because I'm afraid of Huntington's and need to dive in and live as hard as possible? Because I
am going to get the illness, go crazy and impotent and turn into a
vegetable, thereby betraying Mary, deserting her in the most tragic
manner, and I need to prepare her for that desertion, that betrayal?

I give in—in my dreams. To the lovely betrayal. I'm forgiven,
because it was just a fantasy.

"I cannot love a ghost. Let's go make love," she says to me in my
sleep, as I see us having a drink in a bistro on the Champs-Elysées.

"I don't want to play ghosts," I reply. "Not yet." In her eyes is
such desire to live for the moment, to forget and exorcise the poi-
sonous fogs of both past and future, that she is irresistible to me,
someone who is living desperately with Damocles' sword. I imagine
us at her apartment. A whiskey, then another. Soft music in the
background: slightly languid, slightly religious, maybe a little New
Age. Just what two battered people need. I give her a long, slow kiss.
She tastes good: a mixture of the cigarettes she chain-smokes, the
whiskey moistening her lips, and something that must be desire. I
undress her just as I had kissed her: long and slow, delighting in
each part of her flesh as I reveal it. She shudders with pleasure at
my touch. We make love once and then again. I talk about Huntington's, but this time laughing. I go to kiss her again. Suddenly I am
jolted back to reality. "I'm scared!"

I scream it. I wake up panting and trembling. I am sweating. Does
this fantasy mean that I love this woman? More than my wife? No.
Mary is life, her sparkling smile, our children, our beautiful apartment, our future together, our life. But I can only think of death,
which does not altogether make me sad.

Paul McCartney once wrote, "Sadness isn't sadness, it's happiness
in a black jacket. Death isn't death, it's life that jumped off a tall
cliff. Tears are not tears, they're balls of laughter dipped in salt."

How can I tell my wife, the woman I really love, the mother of my children, whom I love, that nothing is important unless you know, unless you feel in every instant that all of this only makes sense because happiness can dress in black, because the all-night party has its morning after, because life comes with death? And because knowing this, you get up in the morning anyhow?

Mitterand, in the end, understood this. Yes, Mitterand the crook, who kept up his friendship with the collaborator Bousquet right through the Nazi occupation; Mitterand the socialist who loved power and money—well, and literature too. As I was detailing all this to a friend, she reminded me of something fascinating that he, that same old crook, said at the end of his life: "Never has man's relationship with Death been so weak as it is in this time of spiritual drought, when mankind, in such a hurry to exist, seem to miss Death's mystery. They don't understand that they are cutting off an essential source of the appetite for life."

Thank you, Huntington's. Thanks to you, I have a goodly serving of this "essential source." Every morning when I get up, I know that death is around the corner. Thus can I face life.

I am afraid.

I am at the hospital with my brother, in the secretary's office. She checks that he indeed has an appointment to confirm that his reflexes continue to weaken, that his neurons are still turning into cotton. I look around me. There is a board with bar codes on it, each one corresponding to someone hospitalized in this department. One bar code is covered over by a handwritten label: PATIENT PUT IN ISOLATION.

Huntington's? Mad cow disease? Why the isolation? What secret is he hiding?

We are early for the appointment. I take my brother to the cafeteria. He cannot walk anymore, or nearly. He constantly twists around in his wheelchair as if someone is pulling on the strings of a marionette. He no longer talks, except to rebel. This time it is to challenge a nurse who addressed me instead of him, the regressing adult.

"Why don't you speak to me directly?" he articulates with great difficulty. His way of crying out for help, to remind people that he is still alive.

He does delight in a few simple things, such as the first swallow of freshly squeezed orange juice. Total pleasure with a capital P. First he looks at the glass. Then he rips open the little sugar package that he—presumptuously—tries to pour into the juice but that, of course, spills partly on the table. He tries again. His aim is better this time. He watches as the sugar slowly falls through the pulp to the bottom of the glass. A jerky grin. A possible smile. Is this happiness? He tries to stir it with his spoon. The spoon knocks against the rim of the glass. Which turns over. Misery with a capital M. Enough to cry, but he can't cry anymore. He can only twist and contort uncontrollably in his wheelchair. That is how he expresses himself. That's how he cries. I order another juice. I try to help him. He pushes me away.

"Stop it," he says in a voice that rises and dips. A voice that is no longer articulate but disjointed like his movements. Finally, he manages with his juice and drinks every last drop. He takes his spoon again so he can scrape the sugar off the bottom of the glass and not leave one grain. His face lights up. You take what pleasures you can in such a miserably unhappy life.

"Good," he thunders to emphasize his pleasure, and to seem like a person who has just completed a very important task before undertaking a new one, such as getting into his wheelchair. But first he has to put his glasses in their case, put that into the pocket of his jacket, which is hanging on the chair, zip up the pocket, tap the pocket to be sure the glasses are there, unzip the pocket, zip the pocket again just to be sure. He takes his jacket and tries to find the sleeve, but he has a hard time. I help him, but that makes him angry and agitated. He still cannot get to the sleeves, and he cries out. This is the first time. It seems to calm him. I take him home. What will he do at home? I have no idea. His wife does not let me come up with him. He told the doctor that he watches television or reads or goes out. I do not believe him, or if he does, he forgets it all very quickly because he never mentions anything to me. So lying to the doctor is one of his last reflexes, just to maintain appearances and to tell the man he is still among the living.

From time to time, I take him to a soccer match. I am amazed that he finds the strength to climb all those stadium stairs, to sit down and be stared at by the other spectators. He is elsewhere. I suppose the noise of the crowd envelops him, reassures him, drowns out the present. He sits in his seat without moving for two hours. He no longer claps or cheers. He cannot clap. His hands miss when he tries to make them meet.

He does not want to come with me to the general meeting of the Huntington's Society of France. But they'll be discussing current research on the disease, how it develops, the experimental treat-ments—fetal neuron transplants (out of five cases, three had hope-ful outcomes; other trials should be coming, and my brother could take part). They will also talk about my favorite obsession: to take the test or not? My brother does not want to come.

"I don't want people to know. Because of my daughter." He is afraid that we'll be noticed, that it will be documented, that we will become "lepers." Bankers, employers, insurance companies. Sure!

There will be over a hundred people meeting in the Salpetrière hospital's assembly hall.

At the meeting someone is at the lectern giving a speech, a report. The speaker occasionally has difficulty with some words and runs out of breath easily. Does he have Huntington's? Already sick? Soon? I look around me. A few seats over, I notice someone twisting about. It could be my brother or my brother's brother. I don't know this person and I know him all too well. But he is laughing. He tells everyone to vote for Jospin in the next presidential election, "because he favors using fetuses for medical research." He takes about five minutes to say this and adds, "And Chirac is against it." Everyone laughs. A sympathetic laugh. What this man just said is not really very important, and, in fact, is not true, because Jospin recently changed his mind. But the man said it and he laughed. Proof of life in a world darkened by death.

Next at the lectern is a charismatic medical researcher. He looks like a calm, wise prophet. He speaks about the five patients in whom he and his team has transplanted some fetal neurons. For two of them, there was no noticeable change. But a third patient was able to ride a bicycle again. A fourth went back to work part-time, and the fifth one began to play the piano again. The researcher speaks about porcine neural transplants, about creating a bank of fetal cells, about preimplantation diagnoses of fertilized eggs that would allow people at risk for Huntington's to have unaffected babies without themselves taking the test. He speaks softly using simple words, a blend of competence, modesty, and true kindness. He reminds the audience that there is no cure but that those who fight are better off than those who give up.

He tells us about some phone calls he receives: " 'Doctor, cure me,' they say. I cannot, but we are working on it." As he speaks, the tension grows in the auditorium. One man, whom I had seen at the hospital with my brother, accuses a psychologist of having been nasty to his brother. A woman speaks about how her husband, who had Huntington's, ended up committing suicide because he wasn't given enough help. "The doctors are no good!" cries someone in the audience. The researcher maintains his composure and replies that few Huntington's patients commit suicide, that doctors do the best they can, that some people give up.

Lunch break. As though it were still possible to eat after hearing all that. Well, it is. Life, death. Knowing that the one cannot exist without the other.

Barbara arrives. She's come to talk about the test—the molecular analysis, the "ogre" they look for in the nucleus of the white cells from a simple blood sample. Should one take the test? Or not? The audience—no, they are not just an audience, they are all involved—the players in this game heat up. Yes, you should; no, you should not; children should... Some people take the lead: "Should, should not..."

"Stop it! Should nothing!" Barbara thunders. "Stop judging each other. There are as many answers as there are individuals. Taking the test is your own free choice. You have the liberty to decide for yourself." But does not knowing go with freedom? I really should take the test... to know.

I play Ping-Pong with my daughter. A moment of pure joy. How could I possibly have this stupid disease? It's so beautiful outside. I can hit the ball back. I can even play with my left hand. My neurons must be working just fine. At the other end of the table is my beautiful, shining daughter. She is cheerful, as always. She doesn't move much when she plays. She tells me she has gotten better, has beaten a boy at school. I play gently, yet she doesn't score a lot of points. She laughs anyway. I laugh. I can't be sick. We go home. I get into an argument with Mary over a stupid thing. She's pestering me about some old TV set that is broken and that she wants me to throw out. I want to keep it, for no particular reason except that I like to keep memories, signposts of the passage of time. My daughter scolds me and says, "See what you did?" She's tired of seeing us quarrel. Okay, I throw out the broken television, say something nice to Mary, throw a veil of peace over our relationship. More like a cloak to hide the misery. I am unhappy. We have such a hard time communicating. I should name aloud the shadow enclosing me, tear it open. I need to know, once and for all, if this damn Huntington's is going to kill me. But what good will it do to know?

Isn't ignorance the same as hope?

I called my younger sister. I am sick of not knowing about her situation with Huntington's. Her husband confided to me that she is worried and depressed, that she sometimes wonders if she, too, will be like Mother. But these are scraps of pretend questions, because the answers are too great a terror. Her husband told me he was tired of seeing her wither and wilt, not doing anything, never seeing people, no longer running errands. And my brother, poor guy, he keeps telling me that she is sick. It must make him feel less alone. They see each other once a week at my father's apartment for lunch with never a word, never a sound, never a glance. Words and glances would be too frightening.

A few months ago I phoned my brother-in-law. I suggested taking my sister to Barbara. Just to talk. See what she has to say about this disgusting disease and how to handle it. He didn't dare. Afraid to face the unmentionable. But you pay for such fears. You pay for not wanting to know, not talking about what haunts you. The result? Something like a heart attack. Not too serious. Just a warning, a reminder from this strange phenomenon called life. Or death. It doesn't matter which. It's pretty much the same thing. Life or death, tragedy or comedy: opposites define each other. As he was getting on in years, the comedian Jerry Lewis was once asked the difference between the two: "There is none," he said. "Is there anything more tragic than a sixty-three-year-old man who spends his time trying to get other people to laugh? And is there anything closer to life than that?"

I called my sister again. Her husband answered the telephone. She was right there next to him.

"She's down in the dumps," he whispered when I asked how she was. His voice betrayed his fatigue, his defeat, and said so much more than the words. What I heard was, "She's done for. And so are our kids. And so am I."

I made sure he had my mobile phone number so that he could call. So that he could talk. So we could cry together. He didn't call.

A few days later he was sick again. This time it was his stomach. Did my sister understand, she who used to be so merry and was now mute? She was the one who telephoned. She wanted to "see someone." I had never spoken to her or anyone else in the family about my own depression. I referred to Barbara from time to time without naming her—this person I don't see often but whose dynamic cheer helps me bind the ties between life and death. And to put up with them. My little sister wanted me to call Barbara right away.

Easter weekend! Impossible to reach Barbara the magician, who has suddenly appeared on my younger sister's horizon. And it's as though she were grasping at this reed that would link her to life

again. With her husband in the hospital, she agrees to have Sunday
lunch at another sister's house. This other sister is older, very stable
and reassuring. A small miracle. But a heart-wrenching moment.
There is my younger sister surrounded by nieces and nephews, friends
and sweethearts—I mean, life goes on, doesn't it?—and lots of com-
motion, but she's all I can see. She is skin and bones. She stares at
nothing. Her twisting fingers grip nothing. Everyone is talking at once;
the desserts are delicious, as always. Her son actually announces to
us all that he is going to get married. His young fiancée is there. She
is gentle, sweet, smiling, intelligent. Beautiful. Does she know? How
could she not know? How could she not see it? My father doesn't say
anything. He just keeps to himself and goes on living. How can he
do otherwise? Occasionally, the younger sister gets up, walks a few
steps, returns to her chair. One time I get up with her. I go with her
out of the room and tell her I will call Barbara, that she will be able
to talk about her distress, that it will do her good. I wish she would
even just talk to me, then and there. It would be a sign that she was
still among us. She says nothing, goes back to sit down, asks Father
to take her home.

"She's got it," Mary says on our way back.

"Do you think so?"

"And you, you don't have it. I am sure of that. I mean, you're a
little depressed sometimes, but you don't have the movements, or
the positions, or the way she looks at things, the way your brother
does or the way your mother looked and acted."

I shiver. Why would I be spared when it was otherwise all around
me? The big brother just ahead of me is sick, and the sister just after
me may be sick, too. And I'd be spared?

"You don't have it," Mary repeats with absolute assurance in her voice.

I look at her. She smiles. How can I be so unfair to her, slightly distant, sometimes even hostile? Easy. I blame my anxieties on her, my terror that someday I might find myself falling apart before her, guilty of disease, a dreadful burden to her, blocking her life and the children's. I blame her for not being able to put an end to my anxiety and despair. I resent her for not being Barbara, who, like me, thinks only about this and talks only about this to me. I resent her because she is not that journalist from my old office who only knew me like this, defined by this illness, and whom I'm drawn to because of this. I resent her for not being God.

I am such an idiot. Because my life goes on, just as it goes on for future heart-attack victims, future cancer victims, people who will be handicapped, impotent, incontinent, all those who are not making such a big fuss over their future illness. They don't know what's coming either. They are going to die, too, and they know it. So damn this stupid Huntington's disease; to hell with it. My wife is beautiful. My life is beautiful, with its plans and memories, its dawns and sunsets, with the smiles of my young daughter, whose body is showing the impending arrival of adolescence.

My little beauty is getting ready to go out.

"I'm going to McDonald's with some friends," she says, and emphasizes the word "friends" with a serious face. She would list them if I insisted. I have no idea if "Manu" is a girl or a boy. She knows I don't know. I don't dare ask. She knows that I don't dare ask. She smiles. The other day she talked to me about her brothers. The older one has gone off to a prestigious institute in the provinces. The second brother will be leaving in a few weeks to study at a British university.

"Isn't that amazing? In a few weeks I won't have any brothers around!" She was neither complaining nor rejoicing about it. She was just acknowledging the passing of time. In her head she must have been reviewing all the good times they had had together. The good times, the bad times she'd had with them, with us. Life together. With or without Huntington's.

I have to stop talking about it. I have to stop thinking about the executioner.



I feel like killing my brother. Just as I would want to be killed when I become like him. An act of love. A death potion. Because he does not want to live anymore, he is not living anymore, he does not and cannot keep up the battle. I was supposed to take him to the saints, those doctors who search and find ways to fight the count-down. A fetal neuron transplant: it might work, and then again it might not, but there would be no harm in trying it. But he does not want to. Something about the timing of the appointment, and yet he is willing to switch everything around for an appointment with a physical therapist or some masseur for his twisted knees. But he does not like the doctor of his brain, that basic matrix, the center of his ailment. One day she prescribes some antidepressants. He refuses to take them. She suggests other ways to fight the advanc-ing disease. He accuses her of using him as a guinea pig.

"Okay, if you don't want to fight this, it's up to you," she said one day when he was again being difficult about scheduling the next appointment.

"Yes, yes, I do want to," he said, like a panicky child. When he got home, his wife scolded him for letting himself be persuaded to go along. She is so afraid, poor thing, and she suffers so, to the point of being unable to think clearly. Her cousin died of breast cancer in the same hospital where they are on the cutting edge of therapeutic research for Huntington's, and she is convinced—she told me this—that they killed the cousin by experimenting on her. But according to her, President Mitterand killed his finance minister Beregovoy, Miss France is a man, and wasn't Diana a victim of the MI5? We face death—either our own or that of others—the same way we face life. She, poor thing, has always believed in sinister conspiracies and that people are basically evil. And this is more of the same. She convinced my brother that Barbara and all the others were not really interested in his well-being.

What idiocies! Or what misery! What idiocy and what misery, both! Because it's just blindness from misery and stupidity that produces such a refusal, such rejection of the doctors battling this invincible enemy. Why turn away from them? Because they fraternize with the enemy, because they spend time with it, they tame it. Just as life fraternizes with death, spends time with death, tames death. That thing against which no rebellion can ever prevail.

Then why not just get on with it and accept it? My younger sister is trying to do that. I took her to see Barbara. What bravery! Or was she simply unaware? At first I did not dare tell her who Barbara is. I vaguely mentioned something about a psychologist, since she is depressed. As we were going, I told her about my own anxieties. I used the word, the big H. She did not protest. When we were with Barbara, it was her turn. Barbara gave the usual little lecture: the gene, the 50 percent chance of carrying it. I could tell that my sister knew all this. We had never discussed it, but like everyone else, she had secretly done some research on her own.

"So what do you think of all this?" Barbara asked.

"That it isn't fair," replied my sister.

Barbara discussed the test but said that my sister first needed to take care of her depression before making any decision. My sister made the usual psychologist appointments and took the prescription slip for an antidepressant, Lexomil. We met up with her husband in the parking lot. He was not expecting any spectacular report. Just as well: we didn't have much to say. But the stress of not talking about it was far worse than discussing it. We hugged each other instead, all three of us. I think he will bear the unbearable better than that other one, my brother's wife. We went to the pharmacy, and they left with their Lexomil.

I'd like to be a coward and not think about this anymore. Zap—my sister, my brother, my nearly ninety-year-old father, who is having increasing difficulty walking. No more cartilage in his hip and no more energy in his head. It is strange how he no longer shies away from Huntington's. He no longer denies the tragedy my brother and sister are going through. But he talks about it with a resignation that resembles a pool of emotions gone dry. His despair has drained away, drop by drop, over the period of thirty years that he has lived with it, apprehended it in every sense of the word. Certainly he suffers, but he has never found the words to express it. Can one really say this about one's father? But he is an odd man, my father. A scientist, maybe a genius, a master of mathematical abstractions, and clueless about how to express his feelings. I remember how he was when he retired—because of my mother's illness. His colleagues had organized a small cocktail party, a mixture of festivity and scientific sparring among the guests. I, who understood none of this and was winding up my adolescent period in great confusion (I wanted to be a journalist to change the world, what a laugh), I was looking out for signs and words of simple humanity and kindness, touches of the sadness that was beginning to settle over him. I could detect nothing but the usual ready-made formulas—mainly mathematical ones—and a sort of awkwardness, an incapacity to send out any signals that I would have been so glad to seize. Just so that I could respond to them, respond to him, tell him he could scream, weep, fall apart—revel in his misery, the better to manage it.

Why did he never clasp me in his arms, even when my mother died, when I broke down in tears before him? Maybe it's my fault. Maybe it is the fault of sons as well as the fault of fathers. After all, I might have—should have—given him some signs of love and affection, too. I should discuss it with my own children. But I feel that I already do. I did discuss Huntington's with them. I even suggested that they could go see Barbara. They don't seem too eager to know more about it. So, secretly, I have written them a letter, just in case, to open and read after I get the results of the test, if ever I take it, or when I start showing signs of the disease.

It was November 1, All Saints' Day, a perfect day for such a macabre ceremony. I wasn't feeling very confident about my dire destiny. So I got out my little notebook.

*Dear all,* I started, to include Mary.
*How strange to be writing you this letter. I hope it will be as*
*serene and reassuring as possible. You should take it that way,*
*in any case, even if it sets off or stirs up frightening and morbid*
*feelings.*

*Well then, I think I have Huntington's. No, I do have*
*Huntington's, because you will only be reading this if that is the*
*case. The beast has invaded me, that beast called Huntington's.*
*Just as it invaded my mother, my brother, and probably my*

*younger sister. But do not be unhappy or sad. And do not be
afraid, neither for me nor for yourselves. It's almost five years
now that I've been thinking about this damned companion,
ever since that fateful summer day, the anniversary of my
mother's death, when I fell to pieces. You were on vacation in
the United States when I became horribly depressed, when I
entered a pitch-black tunnel. For a few days it felt like pure hell,
that place where you feel you no longer belong to yourself.
Anxiety tossing you around, panic manipulating you—no,
that's not true! Never forget this: in the face of death, in the face
of seemingly bottomless despair, facing the inevitable, we're still
the strong ones. For these nearly five years I've been living with
just one word in my head: Huntington's. Day in and day out.
And yet I am living, I love life, I'm having a good time with life.
Do you think I look unhappy? At work they see me as incredibly
energetic and peppy. And every day I am happier being with
you, listening to you, seeing you, telling you jokes, living. The
future? What about it? I 'm going to go downhill like my mother,
like my brother. Little by little, I'll lose the ability to walk or talk.
One day I might not even recognize you. And along the way I'll
make incoherent remarks. And so what? Everyone eventually
goes down that road. What counts is living. And living well. I've
had a great life. Unemployment? Yes, but you keep going.
Problems on the job? Yes, but you keep going.*

*Huntington's? Big deal! It could have been cystic fibrosis,
cancer, a car accident, or the fate of this baby I saw one morning
in a Kurdish refugee camp on the Iraq-Turkey border after the
first Gulf War. It was around dawn. The baby was in his
mother's arms, and he had just died of hunger and exhaustion.
His father gently wrapped him in a towel. He closed this shroud
with adhesive tape. Yes, they had nothing to eat, but they had*

*adhesive tape. He went to bottom of the mountain and dug a*
*hole, alone, without a word, without a tear in his eye. So I tell*
*you, Huntington's? Big deal! Do not be too unhappy for me. And*
*don't go to a lot of trouble over me. As long as I'm not too bad,*
*pay me a little attention: take me to a soccer game, put*
*earphones on me and play some nice music, set me in front of*
*the television, talk to me, stimulate me. And then don't worry.*

*And don't hesitate for a moment to stuff me with drugs.*
*When it is time, ask the doctor to up the dose a bit. Don't let the*
*burden that I am weigh you down, even though I know you*
*have strong shoulders. And don't be afraid for yourselves. Yes, of*
*course, you are at risk and might get this disease. The way I was*
*at risk, the way all my brothers and sisters were, the way any*
*victim of a genetic disease is. But keep the enemy at bay. He is,*
*for the moment, only a virtual enemy. Just like cancer, like a car*
*accident. . . .*

*I repeat: Death comes to us all. All the more reason to take*
*full advantage of what one has and to make a friend, or at least*
*an acquaintance, of Tragedy, another experience that intensifies*
*and sharpens our emotions and reasoning powers. As long as*
*you can, remember that life is good despite these miasmas,*
*whether they be genetic, emotional, professional,*
*environmental. Afterward, when we're no longer aware, I don't*
*know; no one does. We topple over into the unknown. Which we*
*cannot know beforehand. So it doesn't matter.*

*I love you all.*

I wish my mother had left me such a letter with its bits of thoughts
and feelings. But she never knew, poor thing, what was looming,
what was about to swallow her up. Huntington's was hardly known
at the time. She didn't have time to think about it or to talk about it.

I have that privilege. I know what is stalking me. Or not stalking me. I need to know. The test. No, no, later. First I have to keep on living.

Do something, for example, about the woman from my old magazine. She loves me. I know it. She keeps telling me, even now. Sweetly, gently. There is no pressure. She does not ask me to leave everything for her. I love her calm, serene, sometimes combative conviction that life is tragic. And I like her body, which I imagine to be small and fragile. Touching. But it is an impossible passion. I love my wife, everything I have lived and gone through with her. As for ordinary adultery, well, I leave that to small-minded people, with small-time feelings. So I only meet with her at the bistro. We never touch. Not even the usual kiss-cheek hello. An occasional squeeze of hands. Ah, what delicious pain. Sometimes I think about taking it a step further, make the fantasy real. Go to her apartment. A scotch whiskey. An embrace. Another embrace. But it would be betraying . . . destroying . . . dying . . . I'm not ready.

I am sick. I know it. The obsession hit me again when I was seeing the GP for a stomach flu that wouldn't go away. He examined me, said it was nothing, gave me a prescription for a few harmless pills. And then:

"Do you have a fever?" he asked me.

"No, I don't think so. I don't know."

"Next time, take your temperature."

"What next time?"

"The next stomach upset."

"What would a fever mean?"

"A lot of things."

I did not dare ask him, but now that's all I think about. My brother always feels too hot. He knows a lot about physics, so he always talks about his "thermal problems." And I vaguely remember reading something in one of the brochures on Huntington's about the thermometry of the body. I just need to get my hands on that brochure again.

I don't try. Fear.

My stomach flu ended. But my stomach still hurts. Fear.

My legs are rubbery, ready to collapse. I must have a fever. Dizziness. Slight. Maybe I'm smoking and drinking too much. Maybe not enough exercise? No, no, these are signs. I am sure of it. The beast is approaching in its own devious way. Slowly, surreptitiously. It's not abrupt. It lets you think you have a chance. It disguises the early symptoms, hardly painful, as those of the middle-aged man who has gained a little weight, is a little depressed, wants to shake up his life. It takes you for a ride before it hits you, pulls you apart, neuron by neuron, removing your joie de vivre, removing your little pleasures, one by one.

What a bitch. You have to resist. Live before you crumble. Give it your all, as they say in sports. From now on, I take to climbing the six flights to our apartment. One hundred and twenty-four steps. Twice a day, I will do this. I do not stumble. I do not fall. That's a good sign. I must take up golf again. Tennis, too. Resist. Keep getting back up, again and again. Go each morning to place my little rock on the path. Tell the idiots that they're idiots. And tell the people I love that I love them. With a clear mind, go forward. Face the scheduled death. I mean, it's not so tragic. What is life if not scheduled death? As long as you understand that, why not be happy? How can you not be happy? Ecstatic even. Because you become so amazingly lucid. And therefore fantastically free.

Life is like golf. A game you never win. Do you know Bagger Vance, the main character of an American novel, who was a caddy in the South during the thirties? He took under his wing a young golf prodigy whose spirit had been broken by the trenches of World

War I. First he gets him to take up his clubs again, and thus take up a taste for life again. Then he persuades him to play the links gently and to realize that the drama, the accident—Huntington's—are golf bunkers on the course. Once you know that, you face up to the difficulties, you take the risks you have to take, you don't try to hit the hole that's 200 yards off when you know you can only hit 180. One day, though, his ball goes into the woods. He is about to take a penalty and bring the ball back onto the fairway. A safe play. Bagger comes up at that moment and shows him an opening between two trees. A ray of sun comes just at that moment. The golfer tries it, he makes it, makes others as well. He misses a few, too, but he finishes his round happy.

"In this game, you don't win," says Bagger. "You play, that's all. You look for your place on the road." At the end, Bagger vanishes, just a metaphysical figure. The golfer keeps on playing. And living. And looking for his place on the road. When he gets old, he dies on a golf course. Thinking about Bagger. Serenely.

My younger sister hasn't found her place on the road. Poor thing. Is she still hoping? The Lexomil and the other antidepressants do not work. I take her to see a friend of Barbara's, a psychiatrist who is part of the Huntington's team. Barbara is there. She smiles at us. My sister manages a stiff grin. I feel as though I'm seeing my mother all over again. She goes off with the psychiatrist. I hang around in the corridor. Barbara's door is ajar. I enter.

"She's done for, no?" I whisper my question. She nods. I don't even ask her why she thinks so. Depression; the movements, still only slight but noticeable, that would increasingly become uncontrollable; the attention deficit that makes her forget what you've just said. The symptoms are obvious. The psychiatrist calls for me. She summarizes, in front of my sister, what they have just discussed. The test. To take it or not. The current state of the research on treatment: promising but still a long way from a cure. I'm not listening to her. I'm watching my sister with her sunken eyes. I take her out to lunch. It's a nice day. We sit on the terrace of a café. The waitress is pretty, the platter is called Springtime Salad. We talk about our children— I talk about our children. She hardly talks. What is she thinking? Does she think she has it? I pray that she won't ask me what I think. I take her home.

"It's hot," she says. That's all. Later on, I call Barbara.

"What should I tell her if she asks?"

"Nothing."

"And what if her husband asks how the appointment went?"

"You say nothing. I'm the one who will tell them. I will tell her and the person who'll be living with her. Make sure he comes to the next appointment."

"What else can I do, then?"

"Nothing. Take care of yourself."

She hangs up. She has patients to see. Future patients to console, non-patients to reassure. I would love to spend hours talking to her, to ask her, face to face, what odds she gives me. I know what she will say: fifty-fifty. Like everyone at risk. Yes, but seeing me, hearing me speak, what does she think is my destiny? Nothing, I imagine. One day, when she was a little relaxed, she told me that sometimes she and her friends play a game, a contest where they predict who will come down with the disease and who won't. "That one yes. That one no." Before I even had time to ask her, she quickly said that she guessed wrong all the time.

.     .     .

I talked to Mary—about my younger sister and about what Barbara said. She is not surprised. She again repeats that she is not worried about me. That we should take advantage of our luck. What a great woman! She is truly the Rock of Gibraltar. I no longer think about that other woman. I'm not really depressed anymore either, I think. Still a little sleepy in the morning, but I'm facing up to it. I won't win, but I still manage to play, to look for my place on the road. I keep on laughing, getting angry, crying: I'm still living.

We all went as a family to visit my father for a Sunday tea. A Monday tea, actually: the Monday after Pentecostal Sunday, the day when the apostles started speaking in many tongues. Were they speaking Huntington's, the universal language of programmed anxiety and despair? My father's apartment holds too many memories that murmur to me. My mother is here, I can see her, on the other side of the table. She is eating her little muffin with great pleasure. Not a crumb escapes her. She says nothing. Her teeth occasionally shape a zombie-like grin. Soon she will go to an insane asylum. To scream, to die.

My daughter pulls me out of this dolorous reverie. She asks if that is really me in the picture, the cherub in rompers with the big smile and the hair slicked down. The frame holds individual photos of the five of us as kids.

"Oh, yeah, that's me. They called me the Ivory Soap kid, after those ads with a cute little baby."

She bursts out laughing. We look at all the photos on my father's wall. One of them, in particular, shouts its symbolism to me. It was taken seven years ago, at my father's eightieth birthday celebration. That was the day when I first noticed my brother's symptoms. He stands at the photo's edge, already quite thin, with a fixed look on his face. Standing next to him is our younger sister. She is not smiling either. I'm way over on the other side of the photo. On the team of the living? Strangely, this reassures me. Stupidly. As though that could have the slightest significance.... But then, you grasp at anything when you're afraid. I go out onto the balcony. A cigar. What a pleasure! It goes up in smoke, ends up as ashes. Just like life.

My brother has blood on his chin. We are having lunch in the cafeteria at the hospital where I have brought him for his appointment. At first I think he's nicked himself shaving. Then I look closer. He's injured himself trying to cut his meat. With his knife in his right hand he makes large, frenetic moves to the left. He cannot help it. I tell him to put down his knife. He does. I offer to cut his meat for him. He gets angry. It is a reflex, a magnificent one, to resist, always and forever, to show that he's still alive and independent. He takes up his weapon again. Instinctively, I lean away from him. I'm afraid he'll stab himself in the eye. Why is he so upset today? The doctor was in a good mood for once. She is the one who is most active in the research on neuron transplants. She told him he should go swimming to strengthen his muscles, that he should see a speech therapist so his words won't get tangled in his sagging lower lip. She talks like Boris Cyrulnik, the famous psychiatrist, describing the game of life as a matter of knitting, even for those who are well: one move, one word at a time—that's how you put a life together.

"We need to play a low-card game," the doctor told my brother. "For the moment that's all we have, while we wait for better options. There are some promising experiments with neuron transplants. And with certain medications. We'll have some results soon."

Is it that mixture of fatal resignation ("for the moment that's all we have") and hope ("results soon") that put him in this bad mood? He is struggling now with his orange juice.

"Why do they put ice cubes in here? She gets on my nerves with her thing about going to the swimming pool."

His brain is still working, but it is being pulled every which way. My mother went down more quickly and was much less alert much sooner, probably from the medication. My brother wants to remain conscious. Conscious of his misery. What is this life worth? What is the value of this floundering body, emaciated but heavy, so heavy, weighed down by so many internal demons that it no longer belongs to him? From time to time he gets moving, and his demons are right there with him, some pulling to the left, some pulling to the right, forward and back. The legs, the arms—his body has no muscles now, but there seem to be thousands of them, dragging him, jerking him this way and that. It is unbelievable that this is the same brother who could run majestically on the rugby field. He would weave in and out with gorgeous mastery of movement. A beautiful objective: to get around the opponent and reach, as they say, the Promised Land. We were so happy on Thursdays, a no-school day in France, when he, the older brother, and I, the faithful fan, would get on the bus that took us out to the playing fields in the suburbs. The coach, forever yelling, would announce the lineup on the bus. Delicious suspense, but my brother was always on the day's team. He'd put on his clean white jersey and run and run. And me, I would watch him and envy him. And now here he is, broken for good, staggering through what's left of his life. Why bother?

Huntington's! Bastard!

.     .     .

When I find out, I'll kill myself.

Therefore, I don't want to find out. Yet I owe it to the children. To let them know if they can have children without passing on this legacy, this H-bomb. But if I do have the test, if I learn that I'm a loaded gun . . . Unless I do it secretly. Not say anything to anybody. Wait for the results. Then one day tell them that everything is fine. That my depression had nothing to do with this stupid malady. That when I cried the other day in the middle of dinner when we were talking about my younger sister, it was a normal reaction, nothing special. A bit of the blues, nothing to do with the number of my CAG triplet gene markers. That would be great.

But what if I lose the toss? What do I tell the children? Do I read them the letter I wrote the other day? Tell them that what matters is living our lives? But then what—when I topple into the unknown? That's not ours to manage, so it doesn't matter.

I'm dreaming: a Viennese palace, or Berlin. In the early twentieth century, before the great quakes. People are dancing. They seem so happy and beautiful. I'm alone, I feel alone in the midst of all these strangers. The windows are huge. Outside it is raining. I'm frightened. Of these people, of this flood of rain. I want to escape. I quit this enormous room and its waves of waltz music. A long hallway. A staircase, water rising in it—I turn back down the hallway. The palace is pitching like a boat about to sink. Into the ballroom again. The orchestra is playing and the guests are dancing. I've seen *Titanic* too many times.

I wake up. As always, with the big question—daily, bewitching, obsessive. What will be my first thought of the morning—about the bird in the yard next door? My daughter's smile? The smell of coffee percolating? The perfume on my wife's pillow? Or will it be about the big H, Huntington's, my friend, my companion, my executioner. Actually, there is no question at all; it is more a statement.

Like a little tune in one's head, like the air one breathes, polluted or not, with all its shadings of light and heavy. Not a question, no. Even if it's the bird I hear first, Huntington's is always on its heels, my faithful and best enemy.

But you have to hang in there. Remember Einstein: "Life is like riding a bicycle," he said. "To keep your balance you must keep moving." And take it all as a whole: the Chopin scherzo my son is playing—ardent, bold, irresistible—and my sister, outside the French windows, pacing back and forth like a beaten dog and pacing some more. She hears nothing of these swells of harmony, gay, powerful, unstoppable. She sees nothing of this handsome, gifted young man going at the piano the way we must go at life and all it holds. My sister is outside, walking, in the broad sunlight. But she is in darkness. The music stops.

She comes over to speak to me. "I'm not better. I still have this anxiety." I'm ashamed. Because I know about it, and I don't dare tell her that I know. And that I'm afraid too. And that sometimes, to allay my fears, I pretend it's exciting to have this sickness, an experience like no other: to enter full force, head-on, into the dark side of yourself. To know how it is to be disintegrating inside, see yourself being dismembered, bit by bit, losing the use of your limbs, being de-brained. . . . But that would be too simple. We don't know a thing about it, we don't even realize it's happening. It's not an "experience," like the near-death thing where there is a light at the end of a tunnel and you come back to tell about it.

I ask my brother. He moans. I ask him what he is thinking. "Nothing, nothing at all," he answers.

"What would you like?"

"Nothing. Nothing special." He speaks in an irritated tone, as though surprised that anyone would even ask the question. The Tour de France is starting. I suggest that we watch it. We get settled in front of the television. He moans, and then says no more. Laurent Jalabert, his favorite star, wins the day's lap.

"That's good," he says, and then moans again. End of his pleasure. Just a few scraps of nostalgia: "You know what I used to like," he says sometimes, "traveling, on an expense account." Another moan that sounds almost like a snicker. I ask him to tell me about some of his trips. Like him, I've been lost in a few bungholes of the world, and had some good and bad times. I urge him on. I talk a little about Africa and the Middle East. He says nothing.

"But you have some nice memories?" I ask.

"Yes."

That's all he says. Then he closes up again. He has no more pleasures, just concerns: eating, going to the toilet. Every morning after breakfast, he shuts himself in the bathroom for an hour. We can hear him moving about, he hits against the wall, roughs up the toilet bowl. Some days are productive, others are not; but either way, it's because he ate something wrong. And then there's the shower. There is one downstairs and another up seventeen steps. Getting up them is a real adventure; getting down them is a miracle. His scuffed slippers keep sliding off his feet, but those are the ones he wants to wear. He tries to retrieve them, cannot, nearly slips, doesn't slip, and finally gets them back on. He comes downstairs and declares a resounding "Good!" It almost seems that is now the extent of his vocabulary, along with *"Okay, so,"* an English expression left over from his business days. He no longer converses, he just marks the time with his showers, his meals, his naps, this daily routine that is swallowing him up as the malady progresses. Sometimes I hear him at night. I hear the same noises, the same "Good!" and the same *"Okay, so,"* punctuated by moans both high-pitched and muted, like a crying dog. Muffled, restrained plaints.

The real cries will be for later. At the asylum. Horror sometimes comes in stages, in slow increments. For the moment he is just a wounded animal who sometimes goes naked from the bathroom to the shower with all modesty abandoned. His behind has no flesh to it anymore. His brain has no more gray matter. He has nothing left but his misfortune and the misfortune he foresees for others. He says nothing for several long minutes. And then, out of the blue, he asks, "Have you seen so-and-so?" ("He" means our nephew, the son of our sick sister.) He looks like a cadaver." He articulates his words with great difficulty. What he really means is that the boy is already a goner.

"And his sister is seeing a shrink. Did you know?"

Whenever he sees this nephew, he only talks to him about his mother. With great concern. With a certain meanness too. For the nephew is only beginning to be anxious for his mother, for himself, for his fiancée. Why rub his nose in it?

Is it because misfortune, unavoidable for my brother and for others, becomes the only landmark for the victim of absolute evil, his anchor, his sole consolation? Is that what he's fighting for? Because he is still fighting, he is. He walks. He wants me to take him for walks. So we walk along the sea; the dwindling body walks, staggers. First he looks at his watch. He decides to do a half hour. Walk to the third bench on the jetty. Then the return.

"Just so I don't become bedridden," he murmurs. I'm ashamed to think what I'm thinking. Suppose I just pushed him down the staircase. Suppose I helped him to end it all? Death would be such deliverance!

.    .    .

Barbara finally did it. My sister knows now.

"She said I have the symptoms," my sister told me. "Just like that, she told me, bluntly. She thought she'd already told me. I know she never did, I'm sure of it. So anyway, I gave my blood for the test. I'll know for sure in a few weeks." As though we needed a few weeks to know for sure. My sister knows already, but she prefers to pretend that there's still some doubt and therefore some hope. The soul is such a strange thing! Because it is not in order to enjoy life more that she wants to wait. She is already utterly dejected, nothing amuses her, nothing gets her excited. Her son finishes his dissertation and she won't go to his oral presentation. Her son is getting married and she won't go to the wedding. It's amazing how everything fits together. She got married twenty-seven years ago—because she was pregnant, with this son who's getting married now. It was on her wedding day that I first wondered what was the matter with my mother. Her jerky movements, her permanent worrying. I remember seeing her in the garage hanging on to my father. I wondered what was wrong. Her grandson, though, doesn't wonder what's wrong with his mother. He knows.

He is getting married anyway. Why not? I did it, too. His fiancée is very pretty. A brunette, a little on the plump side. The low neckline of her bridal gown reveals her majestic breasts. One could just imagine her as a splendid Madonna breast-feeding the royal baby in a Flemish painting. And will she have children? Has her fiancé, my nephew, even told her why his own mother was not at the wedding? He must have. I saw them together. I saw them with my brother. So is she telling herself that it only happens to other people? The white stone church is in the old part of the town. The tower leans a little, but its curves are gentle and soothing. The stained-glass windows sparkle. The priest pronounces the required words about "for better or for worse." Although he knows nothing about the situation, he even talks about sickness, about the devotion they should show each other. He knows nothing, but everything is provided for in life, isn't it? By the churches, by the elders, by the officials, by the elite. The words of their sermons, their speeches, have foreseen everything; they say it all, don't they? The liars! They don't say anything, they don't know anything, the scientists. Their knowledge explodes into a million pieces when it comes face to face with the horrors of life.

The "big shot" does come. That's my other brother. He is taller, older, smarter. He used to be a leftist—an ecologist, an antinuclear activist. Today some multinational company pays for his research, and all he dreams about are academic positions and prizes. Nothing wrong with that. Still, you'd think this evolution would have brought him a little humility. No! This is the great scientist who told me that our brother's illness was not really serious. "In fact," he said, "they've found some good stuff in monkey trials."

Today he wonders, *Gee, what's the matter with our younger sister? Why isn't she here? I'm sure it's nothing.* As though he didn't suspect. As if he didn't know. He is like the doctor who keeps smoking and coughing and doesn't realize he has lung cancer. Fear makes people stupid. Stupid and mean. I tell him I'm tired of hearing him pass judgment on everyone and that, instead, he might show a little interest in his sick brother, even though that brother never wants to hear from him again.

"You disappointed me," he gets back at me. "Your career has gone nowhere. I expected more from you." I suppose it is his way of handling his own anxiety, his fear of the unknown. I'm not much better at it. I flare up. I, too, can hurt people with my words. One of my sons vaguely hears our quarrel. On the way back in the car, he reproaches me.

"You were way out of line," he tells me coolly. "I was not proud of you."

It is three o'clock in the morning and we are on the highway. The car radio hums—Fabienne Thibault is singing the perfect words: "We tear into each other, we desire each other, but in the end—we realize, we are each all alone in the world." I remember this singer from way back. It was in Montreal. René Lévesque had just lost the first referendum on Quebec's independence. He was acknowledging his defeat and the end of his dream. He came onto the stage, this frail little man who had lived a lot and smoked a lot. His face showed the ravages. She came up behind him and slowly, quietly sang "Aimons-nous quand même" ("Let's Love Each Other Anyway"). I cried, along with about twenty thousand other people. Tonight she's making me cry again. I cannot drive. I pull over to the side of the road.

"Forgive me," I say to my son, "but my nerves are shot."

"It's okay," he says. He makes a vague gesture toward my shoulder. Life goes on.

The next day I learn that my daughter has her first menstrual period, my oldest son has his first job, and my second son has had sex for the first time. I look at myself in the mirror. I'm fat. People with Huntington's are usually skinny. So for the moment, life goes on. Real life. I forget about the other kind, the lives of my brother, my sister, their families. I'm ashamed. For a few days, I don't call them. I do like everyone else: I work up a skill for not caring. I preserve and protect myself. Easy.

.　　　.　　　.

Vacation. America. I have not gone for two years. The New England hills are still beautiful and beckoning. The woods, the lakes in the early morning. "Good morning, America, how are you?" sang Woody Guthrie, the bard for an America that can dream, for the America I love. Woody Guthrie, dead of Huntington's, son of Nora, dead of Huntington's. Like Mother.

So I, too, am Woody Guthrie, who was born in 1913, dead at fifty-four, vagabond of Liberty, wanderer of wide-open spaces and militant of the right to happiness for all. I'm Woody Guthrie, father of folk music, father to Arlo Guthrie, spiritual father to Bob Dylan. I'm forty years old, and because I feel, because I know, what is coming to me, I write: *What am I gonna do, What am I gonna do, What am I gonna do when my shock time comes?* I'm Woody Guthrie, naked, helpless, in my shabby room in New York, listening over and over again to my songs that were mainly unknown and ignored during my lifetime and that will become a cult.

> *This land is your land,*
> *This land is my land,*
> *From California*
> *To the New York island.*

The old record player is wailing, and I will never know that in the years to come, everyone will be singing this damned song: Peter, Paul and Mary; Trini Lopez; Harry Belafonte; Bing Crosby; Paul Anka. In fact, one day in 1975, all the children of America will begin their school day singing my chorus—a chorus by a former Communist—to open the first annual Music in Our Schools day. There's even some talk in Washington about making it the new national anthem. They're crazy! Because I'm just a poor, staggering alcoholic, a drunk; grandson of George, who was thrown from his horse by a devil named Huntington's; son of Nora, who because of the same devil, went around setting fires everywhere. Me, I just write songs. Because I have this thing eating away at my soul and body.

"It doesn't hurt. It's just that my legs, my arms, my hands belong to somebody else. Not to me." I'm Woody Guthrie and I cannot go on. I no longer even have the energy to flail about in my hospital room in Graystone Park, near Manhattan. I have a waxy look. I weigh ninety pounds and I only have a few vague memories. Who is this woman leaning toward me and kissing my forehead? Is it Marjorie, the woman I cheated on, abandoned, went back to, stopped loving, loved again? Marjorie, who was tormented her whole adult life by my bad moods? Maybe. Probably. I don't know anymore. She kisses me. I blink my eyes to show thanks. I haven't talked for a long time. I'm Woody Guthrie and I'm dying of Huntington's disease. I'm not Woody Guthrie.

The scent of Massachusetts in the early morning is the scent of life. The sun shining on the wooden houses and maple trees, the dew on the pine cones, celebrate the pleasure of existence. I had sworn that I would start playing tennis and golf again, and I did, in those beautiful Massachusetts hills. My vision is blurred and I'm short of breath, but my son's lob doesn't take me by surprise. The ball is coming down toward me. Quick. I need to gauge its trajectory and its speed. Jump for it and return an angled shot. Land on my feet. Without stumbling. It's my point. I'm delighted. I've won Wimbledon.

Barbara did tell me that as long as I can manage extensions of my arm, such as a tennis racket or a golf club, I'm not sick—not yet, anyway. Because these are games of skill, sensitivity, and concentration, and Huntington's and the shock waves they inject into your body obviously don't allow you to play them. My golf balls soar straight ahead, high and far, skirting the water on the left and the sand trap placed strategically on the right to test one's control. The sound of my club whisking the grass and stroking the little white ball into the air is a caress to my ears. I follow the ball with my eye as it arcs, then lands gently on a cushion of grass and rolls a few more yards to the spot I had aimed for. I'd like to freeze these moments in time forever.

I'm not sick. (Not yet.) I'm ashamed.

Back there, what is happening to my brother and younger sister while I play my vacation games, my games of life? They are wasting away, they're in torture, they are slowly dying. And me, born between the two of them—why would I be spared?

It's a crazy scenario. Let's imagine this: My mother and father are making love. "Hello," says the sperm to the egg. "Let's go pick out some genes. Now, for the brother—what do you think? I could see him suffer. Let's give him some Huntington's CAG. And the younger sister too. But wait, there's the Ivory Soap baby in between—no, let's not bother with him."

Is that how it works? Help me, Barbara and all the saints! Is this really the way God fulfills his job as Creator? And if it isn't God, then who is it? Chance? Or necessity?

Go ask the expert, the research scientist. He looks like he has a good head on his shoulders. And a small office. Someone told me he will get the Nobel Prize one of these days. But for the moment, he just has a small office he has to share with other people. I speak to him quietly so the others won't hear. You never know. The secretary does not know why I've come, but she knows my name. What if she tattles on me to her girlfriends, to my boss, my insurance agent, my banker? The expert can feel that I'm on my guard. We go elsewhere to talk. I tell him everything about my life and ask him how it works. What about the science in all this? And God? Why my brother and my sister and not me? "For the moment," I add.

"Not me, for the moment," I repeat. Because that's the only thing that really interests me. When will it be my turn? The expert tells me that he doesn't see patients. And in any case, he doesn't have the answers. He talks about the lottery, a throw of the dice, a stroke of luck, a 50 percent chance, the same as a person can be born a girl or a boy. For Huntington's all they know is if you're born with the number 4 chromosome from your carrier parent, that's the game. A mutant gene there has too many of a triplet set of chemicals (CAG) that governs the production of an amino acid called glutamine; at some point in your life, glutamine production goes wild and makes mush of the neurons in the striatum of the brain. Why? Nobody knows. How? Nobody knows. Why does this usually only begin to show late in a person's life? Nobody knows. All we know is that there is a wild acceleration in the death of neurons in the striatum, the forepart of the brain. The neurons in that part program your behavior; if they rot, the pathways that make you behave like a human being are cut off.

"Because your cells shoot themselves," as the scientist would put it.

He is crystal clear. It is almost entertaining to see his schemas and his cross sections of the brain on his little computer. There are splashes of color everywhere on the screen, with clear outlines and then a few nebulous areas where the neurons have turned to mush. The expert has twinkling eyes and a beaming voice. And yet he speaks of horror. Actually, doctors are like reporters. They love illness the way a journalist ends up loving war. And the way we, the living, end up befriending death, or at least being fascinated by it, which is the beginning of love.

He tells me about his research, or about his ideas. For example, putting substances into the brain that might limit the amount of lethal glutamine liberated by the gene gone wrong. But they have not yet found the right substance. One could also try giving the patient more neurotrophic factors, the agents that keep neurons alive. We have about a dozen such agents in our heads. But how can they be put into patients' brains, and in a continuous way? Well, they might be fed in through a little porous tube, the expert continues, half a millimeter in diameter, to be inserted under the skull. It's been tried on monkeys: macaques need two capsules on either side of the brain. A man would need four capsules. But the cells that produce these wonderful factors only live for six months; we'd have to make new holes in the brain every six months. Not so hot. This leaves neuron transplants. If we introduce neurons to a normal brain, they don't connect, but if there's a deficit, the brain becomes more welcoming.

You have to take some fetal cells from the area where the striatum would be developing and, with a syringe, inject them directly into the affected zone. About seven inches deep.

"Not on a kitchen table," said the scientist, "but nearly." That is what he and his team did. With good enough results from six guinea-pig patients to carry it out on a hundred more. Without being overly optimistic about the final outcome of the race between the grafts and the continuing suicide of the other neurons. Because one can't completely reconstruct an entire striatum.

I prepare to leave. But he keeps talking.

"Actually, there is only one real solution: genetic counseling. Allow people who carry the mutant gene to have children who don't. If everyone would accept testing, then those with the gene could have in vitro fertilization. We check the fertilized eggs and implant only those embryos without the bad gene. The disease would be eradicated within two generations."

He frightens me suddenly with his brave new world talk. He can tell I feel ill at ease. "Of course, it is a solution that we cannot promote," he adds. "I've never suggested to anyone that he or she should take the test. I am very aware of what that represents. I know a young lady who, at age twenty-four, had the test and found out she carried the gene. She was devastated. She went crazy. And yet, another woman cried for three days and three nights and then she decided to fight it."

"What do you mean, fight it?"

"Live, just simply live. As well as you can. Except with a little extra baggage. But we're all going to go, right? With or without Huntington's. Don't ever forget this: Man is a sick animal. I think it was Nietzsche who said that."

"I don't know. I don't care." I thank him. I get up. He walks me to the door.

"One more thing," he says. "I no longer see patients, but in my opinion, you don't have it. In any case, not right now. You don't display any of the symptoms. How old are you?"

"Fifty-two. And a half."

"Well, statistically, you're on a good path. We've seen it appear at much older ages, but you seem to be okay."

What a great man. Why would he have told me that if he wasn't sure of his diagnosis, he who has seen so many sick people and so many who will be sick?

In the car I start singing. Fabienne Thibault was wrong. In the end, you're not always alone. Because there are people like this scientist, like Barbara and the other doctors, even if they don't have all the answers; and then, there are the children, even if they do grow up; there is my wife, even if... Even if what? It's true that she is not always patient with me, that she doesn't like it that I snore at night or my immature behavior at times; she doesn't always listen to me or laugh at my jokes. But, oh, how I love her scent! And her laugh when I bite her nipples! And our journey together, even if we had a few battles. A person would have to be really desperate or crazy to destroy all that.

Or sick.

Sometimes I wonder what it would be like to do something crazy. Like leave one day. With that journalist I no longer see. Or with that other one in my office, a few desks down. Beautiful, tall, magnificent, good-humored—I think she likes me. I make her laugh. And my outspokenness impresses her. Not only that, but I think she is not very happy in her private life. I was wondering the other day—we were laughing together at a cocktail party. I said to myself, *Here's a film*. Okay, I tell her, "I think I'm going to fall madly in love with you." She wouldn't answer, would only smile, and she would take me into a corner of the room and tell me quite simply that she thought we went well together. Nothing would happen then, but a few days later, more would happen, and we would go away, we would make love, and then...?

And then what? Nothing, probably, except suffering all around and total incomprehension. Ruins. A person would have to be crazy.

Or sick. Have Huntington's. Know that you are in for it and have nothing to lose.

I feel like calling my wife to tell her all this. To tell her that she has to help me resist. Resist these anxieties that wear a person down. Resist the time that goes by and soils you. No. She would think I was weird, and she'd tell me, as the scientist did, that I have none of the symptoms, that I feel guilty about my sick brother and younger sister, that my soul-searching is typical of all the millions of fifty-plus-year-old men. I call her anyway. To ask how she is doing. She tells me everything I knew she would tell me. How can she be so solid, mistress of her anxieties, mistress of her fantasies. An admirable unconsciousness, and it reassures me. I guess that's love.

*Thursday, April 4: D-Day.*

*Why am I going back over all this? Days are flying past, time is flying past, and the hands on the clock keep moving, and I sit here, immobile, on my bench. Another twenty minutes and things will either stop or move on. Or maybe Chaos?*

*Everything keeps going. Whether you like it or not.*

My brother phones me. I mumble a few embarrassed excuses—work, family, a trip.

As though this can explain my silence for three weeks after I return from vacation. But I cannot tell him the obvious: that to live well, I have to block them out, my brother and my younger sister; block out them and that horrific beast that is eating away at them and that I fear may come and eat me as well. To make up for it, I ask him out for lunch tomorrow. The ritual is still the same. I ring the intercom at the entrance to his building. He never invites me to come up. His wife...she does not want to see me, not me nor anyone else from my entire family. We are a family of murderers, in her opinion. Witches, all of us. Salem and our family, it's the same battle. Another inch and if she really had guts, she'd sue my father. For mental cruelty. Like that guy whose parents sued the French government because their son was born handicapped and they deserved some compensation. Compensation for what? For their misfortune? For the ugliness in the world? For our tragic destiny, inevitably tragic? What a joke!

My brother comes down from his second-floor apartment. He staggers his way to my car parked in front.

"Hey!" He could still articulate this word. One of the last signs of belonging to the community of the living. A familiar word, convivial, for someone who is slowly fading away from this community. We go to a restaurant nearby. We can no longer sit across from each other, for he needs to be able to stretch out his leg, then bend it, then stretch it out again. Abruptly. Like a soccer player's uncontrolled tackle that earns him a red card. He has a new tic: his left temple comes to lie on the back of his left hand. The movement is even but unexpected. It is not controllable, but it happens in slow motion. First he cocks his head slowly. Then his hand comes up to it, supports it for a moment, then drops back to the table. He says nothing. He is like an exhausted animal whose body expresses constant pain, a silent sobbing. He scarcely speaks anymore. I ask if he is reading any books. He says no. Newspapers? He says no. Just no. Television? "Migraine," he responds. Just one word. He only speaks in single words now. Sometimes, though, he will say an entire sentence.

"I have a sad life."

He is conscious of it. Surely, we can help him to be less sad. I want to help him. I ask him the stupid question, idiotic, desperate: "What would give you some pleasure?"

He looks at me. His eyes can still express a sort of amazement. And his brain can still reason. The striatum is not yet a rotten cantaloupe.

"What?" he says.

And I repeat my obscenity.

"What can we do to make you happy?"

"You can't take away my illness," he says in one breath, "so ..."

He will not speak again. Except when we say goodbye. "We'll get together again? Soon?" he asks.

He no longer sees many people. My father, a little, who takes him to the physical therapist. Our older sister, who is retired now and, like me, does what she can. He does not see what's-his-name, his former business colleague, who called me the other day to say my brother didn't seem well. Old friendships, like family relations, have trouble standing up to the stress of Huntington's.

"What's-his-name is not actually very smart," he had once flung out, in one of those definitive declarations so dear to Huntington-ians. He was telling me about a lunch date with the man, who he had probably hoped would remind him of the good old days at the office.

Of course, Brother. We'll get together.


After New York, where I have to go on business. The city has just lost its two towers. It is reeling. The misfortune of others, in the end, does you good when you are feeling bad. I walk around to fill up on it. To share it.

I call my old friend Ben. I met him at college thirty years ago. He had a small, graceful body, blue eyes the color of the ocean, a melodic voice. He was also the world expert on the British Labor Party. What could have possibly drawn him to that?

Anyhow, at that time, when we were inseparable, he became or came out as a homosexual. He would talk around it in our conver-sations, and I would listen. He liked that—that he could talk around it and that I would listen without rushing him, just casual. He liked that I found it unsurprising, ordinary, while he was going through an incredible internal maelstrom. In any case, we remained friends. Close friends, even if we didn't see each other very often. One day, a few years back, he wrote me that his friend had died of AIDS. And now this time, when I call him to say I am in town, he tells me that his new friend has been killed in the Twin Towers. He had been a financial analyst. He was dead. Because some stupid bearded guy, sexually and intellectually impotent, had decided to drown his deficiencies in an orgy of apocalyptic violence. Ben suggested we meet at Ground Zero, the place where tons of rubble had buried his love.

"I need to come here often," he tells me. "Because otherwise this whole horror remains virtual. Just images among other images. Ross—that was my friend's name—called me on his cell phone. He said he was going to try to walk down. I saw the rest on television. When the tower collapsed..."

A month later, the ruins are still smoking. Ben goes to see them nearly every day. He says he does not cry anymore. "Because Death can go fuck itself. Because I have to get past it." He begins to cry. I take him to a restaurant in the Village, on Bleecker Street. I always liked Bleecker Street. Because Simon and Garfunkel made it the title to one of their songs. And because in this street with its boutiques and music, there is an endless celebration of the bottomless happiness of life and renewal, of creating and imagining, of loving and parting; every day, the happiness of being a New Yorker gets reinvented.

I tell him about my misfortunes, at least those of my brother and younger sister. And mine, potentially. Ben tells me not to take the test.

"What good would it do? You can't cure the fucking sickness."

"Yes, but just to know. Know my destiny. That's everyone's dream."

"Yeah, and ruin your existence. Know? Oh, right! Ross, my Ross, when he left for work that morning of September 11, do you think he would have liked to know his future? In the morning before he left, we made love. He left the house a happy man. You actually think he would have wanted to know his fucking destiny?!"

We go our separate ways, saying we really ought to get together more often. "Because you never know, you know?" he says. We smile.

We give each other a hug—a big hug, as Americans say. A real embrace, full of tenderness and a certain unease: these two men's bodies connecting.

I dawdle a bit around Bleecker Street. And then I walk. I'd written down the address on a piece of paper. I don't know if I really feel like going. But I go. I ring the doorbell. It is on a dismal street between 6th and 7th avenues. A warehouse district, potholes everywhere, noisy trucks and garbage bins. Downstairs on the intercom is an acronym among others: HSA. Only insiders, like me, would know what it stood for: Huntington's Society of America.

A voice asks what I want. I don't really know. I end up saying that I'm French and that I need some information. The person tells me to come up. A young woman receives me. A volunteer. There are several others like her. Smiling. Attentive. Listening. We go into a small office. On the wall is a photo of Woody Guthrie. The young woman waits for me to speak. I don't know what to say. She has long blond hair. She still says nothing. She just has her cheerleader-captain smile, her head tilted, and this gaze straight into my eyes, meant to invite me to tell my secrets.

"I was in Paris not so long ago: a beautiful city," she says finally. "My name is Janet," she adds, probably to put me at ease. Suddenly I feel I'm in a meeting of Alcoholics Anonymous. Actually, it is not so unpleasant. I talk to her about my family, ask if there are any books, any people, any hope... She holds out a book with a pretty jacket cover of a beach, a calm ocean, a sunset, kites flying. On the epigraph page is a quote: "True courage is like a kite. Adverse winds help it to fly." The book is called *The Faces of Huntington's Disease,* a series of short stories and poems, all heartbreaking, by patients and future patients, by their families. A series of stories about anguish, about madness and death, suicides and desperate quests for life. And for God. I don't even realize that Janet has left.

She comes back an hour later. My eyes are red. I've recognized my mother, my brother, my younger sister, and sometimes me on every page. Janet asks if I want to purchase the book. I push the idea away as though it were something foul. She talks about Marie Curie.

"She said, 'One must not be afraid in life. Only seek to understand.' That's what she said, Marie Curie."

She talks to me about God, hope, life going on. She quotes Benjamin Franklin, inventor of the lightning rod: "Don't wait for the worst. Don't be afraid of what might never happen. Stay in the light of the sun."

Ah, dear Marie Curie, obsessive scientist, and that admirable Ben Franklin, dreamer among idealists. Not be afraid? Seek to understand? They don't know my mother or my brother or my younger sister. Nor that torturer named Huntington's, who puts the fear in us all, even if it may well never come to pass. As for understanding... Even the scientist doesn't understand. Maybe God does?

I should go ask God.

I continue wandering around New York. The city bristles with rumors of anthrax, dirty-bomb threats, and more planes crashing. And yet the city and its inhabitants are pulsing with life. I go into a bookstore. Looking for, finding, reading books about life. Americans are phenomenal. On one shelf, side by side, will be titles such as *Find Happiness in Life's Lessons* and *Final Exit,* a how-to manual for suicide, a book that would be forbidden in France. I buy them both. You never know. One or the other could come in handy someday. What does the salesperson think when I lay them on the counter for purchase? A book on life and a book on death. Apparently, she thinks nothing. What a strange world. She could at least ask me how I'm doing.

"I'm doing all right," I would say. "So much better than when I closed the shutters that summer when I was all by myself. Four years ago, nearly five since then. I was afraid I might throw myself out the window in the middle of the night without even thinking about it. And at the time, I wasn't even wondering if I would get the disease; I was sure I would. So what has happened since then? For one thing, my psychiatrist is the one who jumped out the window. And me, I'm not even taking happiness pills anymore. I'm still afraid, for sure, but not to the point of forgetting to live."

I saw Barbara again. I told her I was writing a book about all this "shit." And then I took it back. I took out "shit." The word does not apply to me. Not yet. I've matured, since my depression, and since I know what is really stalking me. I feel freer. And more lucid. I know what is important: the present moment, but without selling short two or three permanent things—without neglecting to tell the children to take risks, to tell their mother that she is loved, and to tell certain TV hosts that they are to real life what the smell of diarrhea is to the nectar in the Garden of Eden. As for what happens after, when Huntington's comes, when Guthrie starts to fall apart, "when the shock time comes"... I have to ask my younger sister.

But she doesn't say anything anymore. She withdraws, she sits on her chair, turns off. My brother is still fighting a little, arguing and hanging on to the great questions of life: Do not fall. Eat. A butter croissant? No, regular! Yes, butter! No, regular!

"Yes, a butter croissant, you should have bought that. Idiot. I'm an idiot." He groans. He cries. He falls. What can I do?

. . .

A minor fainting spell to begin with. It happened in my office. The posters on the wall started to spin. If I had been standing, I would have fallen. I hold my head in my arms. The room keeps spinning anyway. Then it goes away. Then it starts up again. And stops. I go to the infirmary. My blood pressure is high: 190 over 100; probably a hypoglycemic attack, the nurse says. A robust, healthy, reassuring woman. I want to tell her about the good doctor Huntington—that's why I nearly fell, right? I don't say anything to her. Hang in there. Put off the deadline. Refuse to see the evidence.

I call our general practitioner, describe the symptoms. He sees me right away in his disorderly office. He begins by asking questions. Why do they always want to know whether your parents are still living and what they died of? I refuse to answer. He takes my blood pressure.

"Hmm... it is a little high. And then, your hypoglycemia," he says. "Your dizziness is a normal reaction." Ah, so I don't have Huntington's. Yet. Unless...

"Stand up and take a step forward and then backward. Do it five times," he orders me.

I feel as though I'm staggering. He tells me to stretch my arms straight out in front. Close my eyes. He checks my reflexes, has me do some tests for coordination, lateral and symmetrical lifts.

"Neurologically, everything is normal," he says.

"My mother died of Huntington's and my brother is going to die of it. And my sister as well."

I blurt this out in one breath. I can no longer keep the secret of my anxieties to myself. I cannot stand it anymore, not knowing, and seeing the disease in my every act, in my every weakness or emotion, and always shoving it away. Because the outlook is too grim and horrible. It's too "not good." I break down, like this morning in my office. Because I wallow in the certainty of this evil thing, and at the same time I hold myself in, hold it at a distance. Some-times I just cannot take it anymore. A person can't forever be both the actor and the spectator of his own fate.

"Ignorance allows for hope," a psychiatrist told me when I was in the depths of depression and had to get away from Huntington's, at any cost. But when uncertainty becomes almost exclusively a source of anxious fantasies, of destructive imaginary love affairs, or of death-wish obsessions, then ignorance also allows for despair.

"Why don't you take the test?" the doctor asks. I tell him what Ben said, about his friend Ross, dead in New York: *"Do you think he would have liked to know his fucking destiny?"* I say it in English to the French doctor. It makes it seem more real. Stronger. But this does not get me any further. If Ross had known there would be that attack, if he had known there would be some survivors, if he could have taken a test to find out if he would be one of them... Maybe he would have made love even better that morning, maybe he would have lived more intensely. Well, I—I *can* find out which side of the fence the Supreme Dice Thrower has put me on. All it takes is a call to Barbara. A prick of the needle for some blood. An appoint-ment with Life. Or with fatal deterioration... slow, unbearable, unlivable.

I cannot sleep. Suppose I just went away. Anywhere. Nowhere. In front of the television. Who was it who said that suicide was the only interesting philosophical question? There on the television screen are two characters about to kill themselves in *La Femme d'à Côté*, by François Truffaut, with Gérard Depardieu and Fanny Ardant. They cannot live without each other, nor can they live with each other. It is like me and my terrible lover whose name is Huntington's. Is he coming again to haunt me? Are my morning dizzy spells some new banderillas freshly planted in my beloved striatum?

Another doctor gives me the same balance tests as the general practitioner. I still have the impression that I'm teetering. This woman thinks I'm just fine. A cardiologist thinks I just have a bit of high blood pressure, the usual affliction of the over-fifty crowd. I'm almost ready to play a little game with all these knowledgeable folks: challenge them to dig into my very depths and find the evil that is eating at me, without a hint from me. Because I know what is happening to me. I know them, these early signs of my soul's tailspin, the beginning of the bodily disintegration lying in wait for me. High blood pressure, the cardiologist repeats. Suppose that's what it is? Suppose it isn't?

"Life is not worth a thing," sings Alain Souchon, adapting the philosophers' words for his own interpretation. Hey, he must be dying, too! This lanky singer is about my age. And his face is definitely ravaged. Yet his voice only sounds nostalgic and happy. "Life is not worth a thing," he continues, "but when I hold my girl's little breasts in my hands, then nothing, nothing is worth more than life!" I burst out laughing! That singer is a genius. I remember the first two little breasts I ever held. Manon! Beautiful, long blond hair. A scent of forbidden adventure. My first party. My brother had taken me to it.

And what were his first two little breasts? He doesn't know. He doesn't know anymore. He doesn't care. He is dying. Without even the consolation—the happiness—of a peaceful death.


It is strange how all the books about death, written by psychologists or by people who claim to have come close to it, talk mainly

about that: the well-known bright light, life scrolling past like a
nice end-of-year TV retrospective, the peace of the big sleep. It almost
makes you yearn to be there. Soft caresses, passions appeased, quar-
rels straightened out, offenses forgiven on the deathbed. "As if," the
French author Marie de Hennezel wrote, "with everything ending,
the whole tangle of pains and illusions that keep us from being
our true self comes undone. Death makes a man be what he was
meant to be—a thing born of death." But I have a friend who
described how his wife died in his arms: it didn't sound like that.
She had leukemia. All he talked about was the morphine being
fed to her so that she would not feel her liver bursting, her stomach exploding. Elizabeth Kübler-Ross managed to define the five
stages you go through before the final stop: denial, anger, bargain-
ing, depression, acceptance. But isn't all that for the dying who
can think properly, the ones whose brains still function? What
matters, finally, is not death. In fact, I'm not afraid of dying; I'm
terrified of deterioration. I'm afraid of feeling shame at the dis-
mantling of my body, my future marshmallow brain, my incoher-
ence, my dementia.

My poor brother—which Kübler-Ross stage is he up to in his
final big sign-off, loaded with his rotten striatum? Which mountain
is he climbing, doped up—or rather, locked up—in the chemical
straitjacket that will become his daily outfit, even on Sundays? It's
funny how we never talked about it while there was still time.
Although death may be such a unique and private experience that
there's no point in talking about it with other living people. Unless
they have totally shed the superfluous things that make up life;
maybe then they can become inspiring interlocutors. Do such illu-
minati exist? Reclusive monks, maybe, living on top of Mount Athos
or in a Patmos monastery, where Saint John wrote the Apocalypse?
Old Buddhist sages filled with Zen? A few Trappists under a vow of

silence? I mean to go see them. Maybe they'll tell me whether I should take the test. The life test. The death test.


I should talk to my wife first. I don't dare. I'm afraid of her reaction to the idea that I might be doomed. Afraid that I might discover that she is not made of the marmoreal material I have always believed. Afraid to spoil what time is left for us to live in the anti-Huntington's bubble that I've built around us. But the bubble is slowly ripping apart anyway. Those dizzy spells... I need to know before I go completely crazy, obsessed with wondering, with not knowing, whether my outbursts of anger, my panicky moments, my bouts of depression, are the first signs of my own apocalypse. I have to go for it, double or nothing. To get ready, to give myself a choice of weapons—resignation, acceptance, or the bullet in the head. Or maybe the entire box of Xanax mixed with a bottle of single malt...a Scottish Lagavulin, or the Irish Bushmills? No, not the Bushmills; that's the drink of the bad guys, the Belfast Protestants. The Lagavulin has a good turfy taste, ideal for a return to the earth. I'll sit myself down by the ocean, in the sand where my mother used to take me when she was young and beautiful and I was a baby. I would scream because I was scared of the water. This time it will be a beautiful summer night—"Starry, starry night"; didn't Guthrie sing something like that about Van Gogh?—I'll be alone with my bottle and my drugs. Or I'll bring along my brother and sister. One way or another, I'll bring them onto the sand. Our uneven steps will leave strange arabesque traces on the beach. We will be dancers from the Big Beyond, choreographed from out there by Picasso or Nureyev or Fellini. Maybe I'll bring music, some Alain Souchon, *"Tu verras bien qu'un beau matin, fatigué, j'irai m'asseoir sur le trottoir d'à côté /*

*tu verras bien qu'il n'y aura pas que moi, assis par terre comme ça...*" ("You'll see that one morning, tired, I'll go sit on the sidewalk / you'll see I'm not the only one sitting on the ground like that..."). After a few minutes, I'll fall over unconscious. The tide will take my body away, toward Ireland or America. The next day it will bring me back. They'll find the three of us, bloated, but at peace at last! People will cry, I hope. Tears of love, of trust in life, worth nothing but that nothing else is worth. For the sake of the little breasts, of little nothings and of the Big Everything, we will, they will, have a great banquet. Like we did for my mother. I remember after her funeral there was a giant veal casserole, lots of carrots, cider, wine. Crying, laughing. Life.

I take a Xanax again, the first one in at least two years. I seem to be alternating now between periods of full-hearted euphoria and equally intense despair mixed with anguish and resignation. Is that because I'm getting near the big tipping point, when the shock time comes? Is it biological, chemical, Huntingtonian? Before they finally self-destruct, the little beasts in my striatum are partying for the last time. I can imagine them, jerking around, fighting to survive in my brain, decaying and thereby stimulating, messily but simultaneously, these atoms of happiness and misery. Maybe they are mocking me, to make me pay for having lived well, thus far. Or maybe, with all the tenderness, sweetness, and energy they can still muster, they are preparing me, kindly, for the Great Beyond.

But to hell with them, those little beasts inside my brain. *Vade retro.* I haven't yet arrived at the moment of truth. I just have passing, natural crises of anxiety, of fear for my brother who is more often delirious now, for my sister who is also digging deeper into her abyss where she can't be reached. I have to resist. Set goals for myself. Thoroughly study my case while I'm still lucid. I'm going to organize a meeting at the Huntington's Association of France, to talk with people like me, see if they are eaten up like me. And I will take Barbara to lunch. I'll tell her I want her to give me stories for my book. But I will only talk about myself. And I will ask her to help me live, then maybe to help me die. I will go see the monks of Mount Athos or Patmos.

Then I think I will be ready. Ready for the test. And ready for the afterwards.

Too late? My old comrade is back. Anguish, ANGUISH, the kind that hits like a sledgehammer, engulfs you, stifles you like a wave.... Three A.M. I've just gone to sleep—thanks to a little pill—barely two hours earlier. I take another pill, a little happiness candy. I go back to sleep, wake up again. A shower. A little cloud. Bad things only happen to other people, right? Xanax, my friend, you are such a master shield against the enemy beast.

I go back to work with an appetite. Hungry to achieve. Thirty years of experience have muscled up a few neurons. "Terrific!" a copy checker tells me when I write a clever headline for a story in the magazine. What does it prove? Nothing. My mother didn't crash all at once either. Like me at the same age, she still pretended, looked good, led her double life while she was already tiptoeing among the shadows. From what I can tell, I'm still on par for her course. She had just turned fifty-three when she plunged to the other side. I'll be fifty-three in five months. How was she, at that stage, a few weeks before the big jump? I could, I should, ask my father. How did he see her then, his beautiful wife he had married thirty-two years earlier, who was turning into more of a shadow every day? Did she have a Xanax crutch, this tiny parapet over the gaping ravine? I don't dare ask my old father. Too scared that he will describe symptoms that seem like mine, necessarily like mine.

Xanax, my dear friend, how long will you keep me going? I'm done for. I know it. I feel it. A foggy shroud is enveloping my brain. I have to tell Mary and the children. They are all home for Christmas. They don't suspect anything. But I must prepare. The letter I wrote to them a few months ago—stick it in envelopes, one for each, give it to them? No. It's still too soon. Why spoil their vacation? And maybe I can last a little longer. I must see Barbara. Quick. She will give me more antidepressants so I can hold on, finish the book, write my last words as a living being, so I can prepare my last real conversations with Mary and the children, sing Souchon to them: "Life is no good. Nothing is worth more than life, la-la-la."

I love you all...so much.

I phone Barbara. The ward is closed, the voice is recorded. Christmas, New Year's. Call back after the holidays. As if you couldn't be depressed over New Year's. Why doesn't she have a cell phone? Why isn't she thinking about me? Just about me?

Actually, I don't really want to die. Even if I'm doomed. I know I'm sick, or about to be. "The shock time is around the corner." Those spurts of adrenaline that alternate with moments of absolute, total despair. Fuck them. I must hold on and bounce back a little later. I just saw *The Buena Vista Social Club*. Those old Cuban men, hibernating ever since Fidel Castro came to power—a New York music producer and a German filmmaker got them out of their prison. They are the ultimate proof of the infinite resilience of man's brain, man's soul, whether or not his striatum is rotten. Live you must, live, live as long as there's time.

Almost midnight. I don't know why, but I called the woman from my old job. To say what? Nothing. Ask her how she is. Nothing more, I know. I still love my wife, only my wife. Then why this phone call, a kind of transgression? My act of defiance as a symbolic homage to the Cuban granddads? Or a call for help?

It is cold. I stepped out of the house to smoke a cigar. It is almost as good as a Xanax or a shot of Lagavulin, my pillars, my crutches of the moment. The lights on the huge Christmas tree across the street have been turned off. Tomorrow they'll take down the decorations. Time goes by, and it gets me closer to my great moment of truth. After the test, when I go to hear the verdict, I'll have to arm myself with one of those helpers whose discovery I owe to the big H. To Huntington's, my friend, my fantasy factory, my scare machine. Intense. Huge. Almost exciting.

The big threat, the threat I'm obsessed with, that has invaded my whole self—am I falling in love with it? I feel I'm on the edge of a huge abyss, but I feel rich, so rich, to be this close to the absolute truth, the curves in the path that leads us to death. What is it that gives me this rich feeling? The uncertainty of the answer? The incredible suspense that has me as its fascinated object? My luck at being able to ask myself the great question in such a harsh way?

Or is this the latest ploy of the ugly beast at work, a mere biochemical process, like a drug that excites and stimulates as surely as it destroys?

I'm sick with my insomnia. Things are happening in my head. I can't relax. An ill-being that I cannot tie to anything but pure, unadulterated fear. It is not melancholy, that peaceful sadness. It is just that I'm frightened, that I hear every beat of my heart, that I doze off into nightmares. So I try to concentrate on other things.

The screen saver on my computer helps—I can see the little bricks piling onto one another in an ideal order. But they look like the neurons of a brain speeding up, little by little, and ending in chaos. Back to the obsession. Quick, something else! List the five greatest movies of all time: *Mr. Smith Goes to Washington* (Frank Capra), *The Best Years of Our Lives* (William Wyler), *Rio Bravo* (Howard Hawks), *Manhattan* (Woody Allen), *La Femme d'à Côté* (François Truffaut)... Nothing but tragedies, or gloomy stories, when here I'm looking for peace.... How about golf? Yes, the great game of golf. Play over, in your head, the courses you've done. Remember every single shot, count them up—what does it do to your handicap? It's almost as good as erotic fantasies. I go on imagining.... The woman from my former magazine, a beautiful stranger in the street, Barbara the neurologist. What would they say if I told them? That I'm sick, probably, that I'm delirious, that the moment is coming. So I won't tell them.

The sun is rising, and I've barely slept. Again. But I have to fight. Happiness is a struggle, a state of mind that you turn on. The poet Charles Péguy used to tell this story: He's walking near the cathedral at Chartres, and he sees a tired man breaking stones.

"What are you doing?" Péguy asks.

"Can't you see? I'm breaking stones. It is painful, my back hurts, I'm thirsty, unbearably hot. It's a worthless job and I'm worthless."

The writer keeps walking, meets another man doing the same.

"Sir," he asks, "what are you doing?"

"Well, I'm earning a living. I break stones. It is the only job I could find to feed my family. I'm happy I have at least this."

Péguy keeps going, talks to a third man doing the same job. This one is radiant.

"What am I doing?" he replies. "I'm building a cathedral."

Where is my cathedral? It's in these daily fights I wage to push off a little bit the moment that haunts me, the moment when, unable to do some simple task, I will say, like my mother with her knitting: "Look, even this I can't do anymore."

Meanwhile, it is still time to fight. Boris Cyrulnik, a French psychiatrist, said: "Only in the storm can I know what I am, what I want, what I'm worth." The Swiss writer Fritz Zorn said he only felt alive the day he was told he had cancer. It is a paradox, but a disease can make you happy, for it allows you to tell others who you are, to make a story of your life. It's what the philosopher Paul Ricoeur calls the "narrative identity": From the age of six on, as soon as you're able to make a story of your life, you construct who you are. But you build it through encounters—with people, with events—swimming, parachuting, getting sick. Happiness in a disease, or in the anguish of a disease? He is right.

Every day I wake up depressed. I'm afraid I'll betray, abandon Mary and the children on uncertain roads. But those uncertainties, and the victories over them, will be our cathedrals. Because the future is far off, and we don't care much about it since we cannot control it. What matters is having, for as long as you can, a present that holds up.

I'm still holding up.

Since golf helps me out during my insomniac nights, I also try it in the daytime. A beautiful winter afternoon. The grass is so green, the people so friendly. The sun, low in the wintry sky, splays out soft rays that remind me of the religious pictures in my old Sunday school books. A little foreshadowing of paradise? I've not played since September. I go to the driving range. I aim at the rugby posts a hundred yards ahead of me, set up to help golfers practice their accuracy. How can I be sick? A nine iron, a harmonious swing... My arms are in working order. The club and the ball click. So do my neurons. The balls go straight between the posts. One of them hits the crossbar. The steely clink sounds like a definition of happiness, the kind of happiness you build in your little daily struggles, in your daily knitting. Huntington's has not eaten me up. Not yet.

Hallelujah!!!

So I talk to Mary. She, too, has insomnia.

"I'm getting obsessed," I say.

"You should take the test."

"And if I lose?"

"You're not going to lose. You would already have shown symptoms, at the same age as your brother and sister. Even your mother had started earlier."

But I know that my fits of depression may be symptoms. Even if I manage to hide them. And my mother had not started earlier. I am about to reach the age she was when she collapsed.

"And if I do lose?"

"We'll see."

She is strong, Mary. I know I will be able to rely on her when I get sick. I remember the woman I saw the other day in the waiting room of my brother's doctor. Poor woman! Huntington's, 100 percent. But her companion was with her, holding her hand and smiling at her. She was responding to his sweetness. By looking at him. I'm sure that, in her rotting brain, a light was still shining. Little by little, the light was going out, but without too many jolts. I think Mary is made of the same rock as that man. Otherwise she would have had enough of me and dumped me a long time ago, me and my often unexpressed mood swings, my incomprehensible grumblings, my deafening bursts of anger.

.     .     .

So I will take the test.

To be a step ahead of the beast. To get the field ready, in case. To learn how to live with it, or against it. Like Arafat with Sharon, de Klerk with Mandela. A man with a woman. The yin with its yang. Life with death. Live with it and against it. Clearheaded for as long as possible.

Was that the magic word? Since I've made up my mind, my anxiety is gone. I'm still alternating between two convictions: I'm doomed, I'm saved. But I can sleep again. A week since my last Xanax. I even went on a radio talk show. A whole hour of lively, heated discussion. I did not stumble over my words. I argued, I made sentences, I reasoned. With clarity. Everybody said I was good. Convincing. With a confident voice.

And I could be sick?

I'm sure I am.

My mouth is dry. So many demons go through my head. I'm going to be fifty-three. My mother's age—as one might say "Jesus' age." Shock time age. I loved her so, my mother. I don't remember that she ever said a mean thing to me. Quite the opposite. I think she worried about me. Because I was not quite like her other children— a little more troubled, not as good a student. She never held it against me. She actually liked it that I went off exploring other territories. A cousin once told me that I was my mother's favorite. And now I'm going to end up like her. . . . I must end up like her. Why not? Like my brother, too, and my younger sister. So what? Everyone will feel sorry for me. Everyone will take care of me. And when I become really unbearable, I won't be conscious of anything anymore. Or I'll already be dead. Because I will have found the courage to use the deadly cocktail of Xanax and Lagavulin. Or because Barbara or Mary will have helped me die. Which I'm asking them to do here, solemnly, of my own free will.

·        ·        ·

I did not dare go to the Huntington's Association meeting, even though I had been anticipating it for months. I had even helped organize it, or at least initiated it. I'd wanted to meet people like me, ruminating over their misfortune, people at risk wondering whether to take the test. I had talked to the president of the group, a heroic woman whose husband's disease was not enough; she had to take an interest in other people besides. I asked her to drum up the battalions of the anguished. She'd done it, maybe thinking of her son, who, like me until now, did not want to take the test.

But then, on the day of the meeting, I balked. I had no more desire, or strength, to rub shoulders with those intimate strangers. Their views no longer mattered. Because after five years of roller-coasting neurons, I have decided to go ahead with it. I left several messages for Barbara. Finally, she called back. I was in a restaurant with a friend, and I could not talk. But she felt the urgency in my voice. We agreed to meet. Set everything in motion. The beginning of the end. Or the beginning of a new beginning.

A blood test.

A few days of waiting.

Soon I will know.

Barbara shows some surprise at my haste. Suddenly, I find her cheek-bones too sharp, her eyes less tender, her hair too coarse, her voice less warm. Because she is resisting me. Suddenly, she is no longer a bridge to my deliverance. The ally is turning into an obstacle.

"What's gotten into you?" she asks. "For the past five years, you were unwilling to know. And here you are now, trying to rush things. What happened?"

"I can't stand it any longer. I'm sick, I'm not sick—I'm going to go crazy. Or get some kind of psychosomatic cancer. I want you to set me free."

"Not today. On Mondays we only test people who we're almost certain are already sick. You're not in that category," she said, looking straight at me. "For people like you, with no symptoms, it's Thurs-days. We don't want to risk mixing up the test tubes. Anyway, it takes a month between the test and the result. And first, before deciding, you have to see the psychologist."

She takes me to her office. As we walk side by side, I look at her. How does she do it, all day long, dealing with our terrors, and not hate us all? She smiles at me. I respond, but with reserve. I no longer feel like waiting.

I already know the psychologist. I saw her once or twice in the weeks after my first big fall, almost five years ago. I remember that she listens well.

"Why do you want to take the test?"

I describe my life over the past five years. She interrupts.

"You're not answering me. Why now? You never wanted to before."

"To have it over with. Because I have all the symptoms. I'm afraid, depressed, anxious, shattered."

She stifles a little chuckle. "You have no symptoms. Your anguish is specific, rational, it makes sense. The anxiety in Huntington's is not like that—it's empty. You may carry the gene, but so far you are only sick from the threat. You've even constructed your whole life, and your inner life, around it. How will you manage the absence of the threat if it turns out you don't carry the gene?"

"I'll party, every day."

She laughs again. "You think it's that simple? For twenty years, your fear has been the fulcrum of your life. If you learn that you are safe from the disease, you'll suddenly be faced with a huge emptiness. You'll have to fill it. It's very complicated. And if you *do* carry the gene, what do you do? Some people in your situation... once they learn they have it, they develop the symptoms in one week. I knew this one woman—she was pretty, elegant, lively. She wanted the test. She did have the gene. A week after she found out, she looked like a streetperson. Other people, they learn they don't carry it—and they break down, too. Have you thought about that?"

"Constantly. In fact, that's all I do. And I can't stand it anymore."

"Well then, what's your plan for your life? If you *are* a carrier?"

"I don't know. Kill myself. Write. Leave my wife. Or love her more, and better, like she deserves. Tell the truth about politicians and journalists, about show business, about TV people. Turn into a serial killer."

"Would you be serious for a minute?"

I exploded. "Serious, me?" I started yelling. "What are you talking about? How can I be serious as long as I don't know? Plan, you say. My *plan for life*? Did you ask my brother, my sister, about their plans for life, their battles every second, every battle lost because their brains are mush?" I snorted. "Don't be hypocritical—ask me about my plans for death." Then I cried.

She said nothing. Her silence calmed me down.

She spoke again. "And if you don't carry the gene?"

"The same. Except for serial killer. And suicide. That would be too dumb."

"Your wife—what does she think?"

"She's glad I'm taking the test. And she thinks I haven't got it."

"Why don't we ever see her? She's quite the ghost, your wife. Is it to protect her that you never bring her here? You think you're sparing her, but you're doing just the opposite. Whatever the result, your life is going to change. A lot of turmoil. For you both. You have to really prepare for it, so we have to see you both, together. Come again, a month from now, with your wife. Then we'll do the test."

A month. Another month. Plus a few days to think it over, I imagine. And a few more weeks till the result. At least.

"Trust us," the psychologist says. "We have some experience."

I tell Mary about my conversation.

"At last, "she says. "They finally discovered that I exist."

I am startled by her tone, and her words. I had never felt that she wanted to come with me to see Barbara. Unless it was I who didn't want her to want to come. In any case, she agrees about getting it over with. Because sometimes, she says, "I don't know who you are anymore."

Mary offers to drive me to the airport. I'm going to Greece for a few days. Alone. She must be a bit resentful. Because she does not understand anymore? Or because she understands too well. She knows I'm yearning for an escape, any escape. From my fate, therefore from her, even though she is certainly ready to fight along with me. I always underestimate her. I should apologize for making her go through such turmoil. On the way to the airport, we don't talk much, but it is a peaceful silence. Before I leave the car for check-in, I kiss her as I haven't done in a long time.

I explain. I reassure her. Why Greece? Why Patmos? Actually, I'm not really sure what I'm looking for. Religion has never fascinated me much. The priests of my childhood, their black robes shiny with wear, their scary holy scriptures, their threats if I didn't confess enough. . . One day, though, a friend told me about monachism, a practice born in the Egyptian deserts in the fourth century—about those men "drunk with God" who made up their minds to die to the world, the ones who pretended madness and transformed themselves into human refuse, those "athletes of exile," "companions to the angels," who stripped life to the utmost to get to their deepest core, to find what was transcendent in them, what was divine in themselves.

Before my big shock time, before the kickoff to my possible withdrawal from the world, before my own private apocalypse, I wanted to speak to them. To find new landmarks, to listen to another word, perhaps to steel myself against the unspeakable. To go a little bit beyond myself. Why Greece? Because in Greek monasteries, there are still some "athletes of exile." Why Patmos? Because of John, Jesus' favorite, banished there by the emperor Domitian. In Patmos, say the religious experts, John saw "beyond the turbulence generated by the beast and its demons, of the scintillating walls of the new Jerusalem." So he wrote the Apocalypse there, the revelation of revelations, from the Greek word *apokalypsis*, which means "the unveiling." Deliverance.

*I, John, your brother and companion in oppression and resistance in Jesus, I found myself on the island they call Patmos.... On the day of the Lord, I was inspired, and I heard a huge voice behind me, like a trumpet.... I turned around, and I saw ... one like a son of man clothed with a long robe and a golden belt around his waist. His head and his hair were white as white wool, like snow, his eyes like a flame of fire, his feet like burnished bronze from a hellish furnace, his voice like countless rivers ... His face was like a sun shining with absolute brightness. When I saw him, I fell to his feet as though dead. He put his right hand over me, and said: Fear not; I am the first, and the last, I died and behold, I am alive forevermore: I am alive for eternity, and I hold the keys to Death and to Hades.... Fear no more what you are going to suffer ... The fifth messenger blew his trumpet; and I saw a star fallen from heaven to earth. He was given a key of the shaft of the bottomless abyss ... From the shaft, smoke came out like from a great furnace.... Then, from the smoke, locusts jumped onto the earth, and they were given a power like the power of scorpions of the earth. They were told to harm the men who do not have the seal of God on their foreheads. They were given the power not to kill them, but torment them..."*

Huntington's, the locust of our own torments... Because we do not have the seal of God on our foreheads?

The sun shines bright on Patmos. The monastery, a gray fortress, overlooks an island of little white houses, blue coves, olive trees, and bougainvilleas. The "angels' companion" is expecting me. My friend told him that I was on a painful quest and in revolt. The monk says that illness is an icon to demonstrate the oneness of all mankind, to show that each individual exists in communion with all others. "No man," he argues, "can say, 'I'm alone, with no relation to Creation.' My problems, my tragedies, are not only mine; they belong to all mankind. When you understand that you exist together with all of Creation, you understand that life is not given for enjoyment. Good and evil, happiness and misery, are not the end goal of life; they are the spiritual beginning of eternal life."

I counter that the slow suffering of my brother and sister are unbearable, unacceptable.

"Brother Jean," he says, "I'm sorry. I do not know the mysteries of God. Every man who is in pain is on the road of the holy martyr. But you will not find the big answers in philosophy or in theology. You will find them in liturgy, in the transfiguration of life and death. You must open up your heart to God's grace."

He stands up, embraces me, tells me that he will pray for my brother and my sister, and for me.

.　　.　　.

I stand there at the harbor like a fool, dumbstruck, or in wonder-ment. The sea is calm. The houses take on a purple hue as the sun sets. Eternal hymns rise out of a small white church. Old bearded islanders are waiting. Waiting for death, which does not come. For the Apocalypse, which does not come.

The boat takes me back to Samos, the neighboring island where you board the plane to return to Athens. The harbor village is called Pythagorio, because it is the birthplace of Pythagoras, a great scientist who believed not only in the square of the hypotenuse but in metempsychosis as well. Life is not simple. Near the village are the ruins of the oldest-known Greek temple, 2,800 years old, dedicated to Hera, the goddess of fertility. Thus I'm in the kingdom of science, fertility, eternity, and God's grace. It is January. The sea is at peace. The air is soft and sweet. The orange trees are heavy with their fruit. If I had imagination, or inspiration, I would say that God exists, that I met Him on Patmos. More modestly, more paganly, I persuade myself that my fears don't weigh an ounce next to this boundless beauty and faith. I forget the god Xanax. I register images, noises, smells, and the sound of the monk's voice as weapons that will serve me when they draw my blood to find out if the locust of my apocalypse is resting there.

I'm exhausted. As if the decision to take the test has used up all my energy. I would like to hibernate like a bear. Fade away in a little death, then wake up in the next stage, after the blood. After the analysis, after the verdict. But I must wait. The meeting with the psychologist and Mary, two weeks from now. The blood test, a few days after that. And another month for the result! I cannot believe it is just a matter of overbooked schedules. The doctors are making me wait to test my determination to go through the whole ordeal. I won't disappoint them. A friend dedicated her latest book to me—she knows about it all: "To my professor of courage," she wrote. Courageous, me? It's just that I cannot do otherwise. And I'm not all that courageous. For example, I cannot bear the idea of facing my brother or my sister as long as I don't know my own fate. I don't call them anymore. My brother called me, though. There was animal pain in his groaning words. "When...you...lunch...with me?" We agreed on a date. As far off as possible. My older sister and my father see him more regularly now, more courageously than I. My father will soon be eighty-eight. He says it is harder and harder for him. But he tries to maintain the ties, the forms. He must feel a little guilty. And totally powerless. So must my big sister. I have not told them that I'm going to take the test. I don't know why. We are such a secretive family. A bunch of emotional dwarfs, quadriplegics even, unable to express feelings. No doubt we would fare much better if we gathered, once in a while, to cry together, to see the psychologist together, to take the test together. But it's as if we were ashamed to share, to expose our memories and fears.

Thank God, there is Mary. "There is no such thing as love," someone wrote. "There are only proofs of love." Ever since she has known that we were going to know, I can tell that a weight has been lifted from her. And I only remember her proofs. Proofs of her strength, her class, proofs of her love. I remember being on a plane we thought was going to crash. It barely touched the ground and then lifted off again. Not a word from the pilot or the crew. Inside the cabin, silence, cold terror. I thought we were heading off to crash somewhere else, in some empty area where there would be no damage for people on the ground. I was shaking. Mary had gripped my hand. She did not say a word, simply closed her eyes. She seemed unflappable. Firmly in control of herself. When we finally landed, everybody clapped. She simply gripped my hand a little tighter. She looked at me. Just a look. Not a word. Everything was said. And then there was this other time. A fire in the apartment just below us, at dawn. I grabbed the kids, rushed down the six flights, reached the ground floor in my pajamas and barefoot in all the broken glass. Ridiculous. She took the time to put on her shoes and a bathrobe, collect a few important papers that would be useful if our apartment had burned. Again, just a look, a look of quiet strength, quiet love. One final story, a last "proof." One of our children, as a baby, managed to climb onto the ledge of an open window. He was sitting at the edge of the abyss, four stories up. My back was turned to the window, and Mary faced it. Two catlike strides—a controlled flash—and the baby was in her arms. Safe. Before I even realized what was happening. That time there were a few tears. Of relief. Of relieved love. That's my Mary, my iron ally in the typhoon, my woman, my wife. How could I ever doubt?

We are facing the psychologist, but I look at Mary beside me, in profile, straight up in her chair. She is beautiful: her high, slightly curved forehead, her perfect nose, her pitch-black shoulder-length hair brightened by a few gray threads of well-mastered maturity. We had met up earlier in a café next to the hospital. I was a few minutes late. When I stepped out of the metro station, I saw her from across the street. She was drinking a *grand crème*—a *"gouand couème,"* as she still said with an accent despite her thirty-year use of the French language. I stopped for a moment before I joined her. I wanted to watch her without her seeing me. To try and decipher what she was thinking as she read her magazine.

I did the same thing thirty years earlier, in a Latin Quarter bistro. We had known each other for a few weeks, and I had fallen madly in love with her, her very long hair, her accent ordering a *"gouand couème."* She talked about her studies, about America and Americans, some of whom she found hard to stomach, and about France and some French people she found hard to stomach. She loved me, too, without really knowing why. "The way you walk," she said once, laughing. "Also, I think you'd make a great father. I'm hooked." I didn't quite understand. "Like a fish, you know, caught on a fishing hook..."

But she had to go back to the States while I stayed in France to prepare for an important exam that would make me a boring English teacher. For a few seconds, without her noticing me, I watched this long figure of a dark-haired woman who looked like the woman in Whistler's painting *Symphony in White, No. 1.* I was wondering what was going to become of us. A few minutes later, I asked her.

"I don't know," she had answered. Tears came to my eyes. Her grip grew tighter on my arm. Already then.

Thirty years later, here we are again, in a Paris café. She looks up when I arrive. She smiles. She has been so friendly since I decided to take the test. And loving. I tell her that. I thank her for being there, as she always is when life gets tough. I repeat that the psychologist wants to see if we'll be strong enough to go through this obstacle course together. She does not say anything, just "Let's go." We go.

"I'm very happy to see you together here, at last," the doctor says. We feel as though we are standing before a mayor about to marry a young couple. "This means that you're prepared to support your husband." Mary nods, her head slightly tilted. That's what she does when she is paying close attention. She is not nervous. I am. The psychologist asks me if I'm still determined to take the test, to cross the threshold of my anxiety.

"More than ever. I owe it to the children. I owe it to Mary. And I owe it to myself. I have to know. To move on to other things. Get loose from my anguish. Since I made up my mind, everything feels better. I can keep the beast at a distance. My relationship with Mary is more relaxed."

I look at my wife as I say it. She flickers a little smile, says nothing, nods.

But the doctor is relentless. She explains that nothing is sure, that I still have a fifty-fifty chance of carrying the gene even though I'm on the descending slope of the curve.

"You understand? What your wife thinks of you, how she'll look at you, will change if we learn that you are a carrier."

"Of course it will. But I'd rather have it change now, while I'm still functioning, than when the sickness hits."

I'm no longer looking at Mary. I don't dare. The psychologist talks to her.

"And you, you will resent him. You are his children's mother. He will have left them something awful."

I still don't dare look at Mary. Obviously. The hypothesis is not new. I've been ruminating about it for years. But the unspoken, when spoken, is terrifying.

"I'm convinced he does not have it," Mary says. "I would feel it. I would know."

"You know nothing," the doctor replies. Her tone is not aggressive, just clinical. "The disease can start very late."

My face is on fire. Silence has filled the room. Mary breaks it. "Yes, probably, I will resent him a little..."

She is looking straight ahead. Her voice is calm. She hesitates for a second. "But it's not as if we had never known," she resumes. "It's not as if I didn't know that we were taking risks having children. We were young, a bit unthinking. But we knew. I knew, even if we probably never talked about it thoroughly, and maybe we should have.... And anyway, you have to die of something."

"So what will you do if he has the gene?"

"I don't know. We'll enjoy what's left ahead. We'll travel. We'll talk to the kids..."

Mary is magical.

"Will you come with him to hear the result?"

"Of course. Can you imagine otherwise, me waiting by the telephone? Of course I'll be there."

Mary is magical.

I tell her so as we walk out of the hospital. She thanks me for the compliment. Where does she get such strength? From her absolute conviction that I don't carry the cursed gene? From a few generations of American Protestant culture—thorough, stubborn, practical, resilient? From her feminine power, the power to give life? Why haven't I shared my anguish more with her? Probably my fear of confronting fear. Idiot reflex! I could have spared us a few storms.

Today is the day. Blood day. The test... *THE test*. One hour from now. How to dress for it? Badly, of course. Old navy blue corduroy pants, shapeless, dirty. A black shirt, no tie. A red sweater. A brown jacket. Black shoes, unpolished. Dramatically lousy. On purpose. It's stupid. But I tell myself I have to look lousy. If I dressed nicely, I would be honoring the demons. It is raining, of course. And I have a runny nose. Just as well. It was easier to call my assistant, claim I'm sick, and come in late. No way would I tell her what I am actually doing.

As she left for work, Mary said, "Good luck with your blood."

"Thank you," I grumbled from deep in the bed. I was neither relaxed nor tense. Just mumbling. In a hurry to get it over with, to end the thing.

Yesterday I had lunch with my brother. The psychologist had told me not to; she thought it would make me panic all the more. That's why I did it. A trial I wanted to impose on myself: proof that my brain is still functioning. When he stumbled out of the elevator, he handed me a plastic card. Like a trophy. He didn't say a word, but he looked strangely self-assured. It was a special pass for disabled people, the sign of a new status. He can put it on the windshield of a car in order to park anywhere. It's years since he stopped driving. But it was a gift from him to us, the living. A victory for him, who clings to anything to demonstrate that he is still alive. A little. So little. He whispered that he no longer does a thing at home and never goes out except to eat, like today, with me. His words are nothing but long rough sounds. Once in a while he has flashes of lucidity. He says that his doctor, the other day, thought he didn't look good and increased his medication doses. The pills knock him out, but they do relax his jerky movements. He still has strength enough to see that our younger sister is worse off than he is. He adds that our older sister does not look sick.

"You healthy ones," he stutters. I stand somewhere between infinite compassion and irritation. I don't dare tell him that I'm going for the test precisely to find out whether I've won or lost in this huge lottery among the (still) healthy ones. I'm afraid I'll make him even unhappier. Because I still have some chance.

A friend left a message on my phone. She wishes me luck, says that compared to all this, our little daily worries are pretty insignificant. She is right. When I get to the hospital, so-called angry workers are handing out leaflets: A 35-HOUR WEEK FOR DAYTIME LABOR! 32 HOURS FOR AFTERNOON WORKERS! 30 HOURS FOR NIGHT WORKERS! I turn down a leaflet held out to me. One man tries again. I push him away, without annoyance, and he moves on. Inside, a poster announces a lecture by a psychologist: TELLING THE TRUTH TO YOUR PATIENTS. That is more to the point for my day. The truth. I'm getting close.

Barbara is just back from a ski trip. I say something nice about her tan. She smiles. I'm also tempted to say that she must have just gone to the hairdresser. But she has a huge talent for sticking to the professional. Totally professional. I'll have to ask her, someday, how she manages to distance herself from it all. Do doctors sometimes cry, thinking about their patients?

She asks me if I know everything I want to know before the blood test. She goes over the old story of the CAG triplets, the chemical elements in a gene that code production of the protein glutamine, how in Huntington's patients there are too many of these triplet sets, and they produce too much glutamine, and it messes up the brain... I give her a nod: Could we proceed, please? She hands me a paper to sign, by which I acknowledge that I, not anyone else and by my own free will, have asked to take the test. She hands me a pen, the depressing, ubiquitous ballpoint pen of the civil service. I ignore it and reach into my pocket for my own Pilot Pen; its very fine point, its comfortable slide on the page, will surely change the whole outcome. If a black cat happened to go by, I would not sign. If I saw a ladder outside, I would go and walk under it. I'm not afraid. I'm even kind of excited. I can see myself in the same office four weeks from now for the result. I can't help but ask Barbara: "What are you like when you give out the result? I'm sure your face says it all, even before you utter one word..."

"First I say hello. And when I say hello, I always smile. Even if the news is not good," she laughs.

What a strange encounter! Here I sit with this woman, to share the most important moment of my life, and everything seems so smooth, easy, ordinary. We are not equal. For me, it is the moment of truth. For her, I'm just another patient. Luckily for her. She could not survive otherwise. Yet she still asks me how I feel.

"Fine. Oddly fine, in fact. Since I've made up my mind to go ahead with it, I don't need Xanax anymore."

"What odds do you give yourself?"

"What do you give me?"

"Fifty-fifty. Like everybody else in your situation."

"If I showed the symptoms, would you tell me? Like you told my sister?"

"You have no symptoms."

"My depression?"

"You have good reasons for depression."

"So I'm going to win?"

"Fifty-fifty. Some people start the disease after they reach sixty. You still have time. Only the blood test can tell us."

She leads me to the room where they will draw my blood. It is the secretary's office. Secretary and nurse. On the wall are the usual postcards sent by colleagues from some sunny spot, children's drawings, and the phone number of the resuscitation team. A few people walk in and out. It does not seem very solemn. But what did I expect? A leather-clad Cruella, with Wagner music in the background and sinister shadow puppets of the Grim Reaper? It's just a blood test.

I stare at the needle as it goes into my arm. How nice it would be to hypnotize the syringe, tell it to draw only clean blood with no Apocalypse locusts in it. The nurse fills up one tube. Another. I ask her where they analyze it. She says the DNA is extracted here, but they analyze it elsewhere. I ask her where. She won't say. As if she feared I would go and break in trying to find out early.

"Now, are you going to be anxious?"

"This thing has been eating me up for twenty years. Ever since my mother died. Now, finally, I'll know." I flash her a valiant smile.

Barbara comes back to wish me luck. We make an appointment for the verdict. The sentencing. Four weeks later. April fourth, a Thursday. In my datebook, I write, "D-Day." Because that is one of the finest dates in the history of mankind. And because Barbara's surname starts with a D.

"Don't phone me ahead of time," she says. "I will only have the results the night before."

Is she lying?

It is sunny outside. I call Mary. Tell her about D-Day. It's 1 P.M. The countdown is beginning. I will start it in the café across the street, with my favorite meal: pork rillettes and pickles on a baguette. With a Coke.

"A Diet Coke?" the waiter asks.

"No, absolutely not. Today is a big day. Give me a regular Coke."

*Thursday, April 4: D-Day*

*That was a little less than a month ago. And now the hour has come. Fateful. Fate. I don't know what to think anymore. I would like not to think anymore.*

The irony now would be to die before April fourth. A car crash on the Paris ring road, a heart attack—boom, so long! Why not? After all, I've done what I had to do, as a man, a father, a husband eager to know for his own sake and his loved ones'. I filled two vials with blood and fulfilled my duty. I'm no longer needed for a decision on my fate. By the way, what have they done with my vials these past three days? Where are they, those two miserable inanimate objects that contain the future of my soul? My whole life is in there, my bottomless anguish, my futureless future or my dazzling redemption. Are scientists already busy with them, dissecting the fuel of my life and death, taking it apart, meticulously, mercilessly? Of course not. Today is Sunday. Scientists have the day off. My two dumb test tubes must be lying on a shelf in the corner of a lightless room in some hospital lab. Me, I'm crying in some lightless room. A movie theater where my daughter took me. A splendid melodrama. It tells the story of a man who starts off badly: In the first five minutes, he loses his job, feels sick, finds out he has cancer and only four months to live. His ex-wife despises him. Their son has rings stuck in all over his body, wherever holes can be pierced. Ninety minutes later, the hero is dead. But he has built a gorgeous house on the Pacific Coast. His ex-wife loves him again. And their boy has become a good kid. I cry over all those wonderful and horrible people, happy and depressed, alive and dying, dead and alive. I also cry over myself, obviously, over my suspended sentence, a living man condemned to death. Like Kevin Kline on the screen, like six billion living human beings.

Only twenty-five days left. Twenty-five more days. Yesterday Mary asked me if we were going to make plans to celebrate on April fourth. Celebrate what? A resurrection? A death date? Deliverance? Mary does not rule anything out, especially not a death sentence, but she goes forward, head up, shoulders back. Amazing. Lucid. It's odd. And inspiring. In these few weeks, we've found each other again. United, to not panic, to not upset the children. None of them knows I've taken the test. We will not tell them. Not until three weeks and four days from now. Then we will celebrate . . . Maybe . . . I don't know now what odds I'm giving myself. Actually, today, right now, I know that I'm spared as definitely as I knew I was doomed when Xanax was the pivot of my life, my lifesaver, my drug. I've not touched it for almost two months. The doctors and my friends tell me I don't have the symptoms. And for my brother and sister, they had started younger. But for my mother, they'd started older. Besides, *what* had started younger, or older? I told Barbara the other day: If we find out that I do carry the gene, then these past five years of on-and-off breakdowns will be seen as early signs, won't they? She disagreed only faintly, I think. I don't remember. I can't remember anything. I can only wait, close off. Lose myself in mindless, pointless diversions. To forget the real questions. Pascal, the philosopher, condemned that. What an imbecile! There's a soccer game on television. Go, *les Bleus,* go!

When I woke up this morning, my terror-o-meter was a little high. Nothing too serious for a Monday. Still ... I counted my Xanax pills in the cloth satchel I drag around wherever I'm going. I've got seventeen left. I should have asked Barbara for a new supply. With less than one per day, I can't really afford any serious anxiety attacks. But I hold on. Resilience. Survival instincts. I even make plans for after April fourth, agreeing to business lunches and cocktail receptions. As if nothing was going on. As if, afterward, everything would be the same. Of course, I cannot behave any other way. But it feels like I'm leading a double life. Hiding the heart of the matter from all those people I encounter all day long. Am I a sick man crouching behind a healthy appearance? Or am I a hypochondriac, bursting with potential health, ill with ugly fantasies? I have to get out of this double agent's life. I don't want to end up like that old spy I met several times in Moscow. I even came to like him. He had betrayed his country, England, his wife and kids, for the cause of the "great" Soviet Union. But toward the end of his life, he could not bear himself anymore. He could not bear his alternate self. On the plastic tablecloth of his pathetic little kitchen, surrounded by pictures of the homeland he would never see again, all day long he gobbled up little pills that looked like Xanax. To reconcile his one self with his other. Or to kill them both. Is that how—in chemistry, in madness, in ultimate violence—is that how you finally settle your accounts with the demons that haunt you?

Only twenty-four days left before my own appointment with the demons haunting me. Will they be alive? Or dead?

Startled awake. The green digits on the clock say 3:58 A.M. I don't remember my dream. A vague impression of being harassed by bug-eyed kids, in a schoolyard during recess. I'm not very old either, in the dream. I must be obsessed with my kids, afraid to leave them with a truly shitty legacy. Mary is asleep. I can't wake her up. What would I tell her that she hasn't already heard a million times? I put on my headphones and listen to the radio. An old Dylan song is on. Reminds me of Woody Guthrie, which brings me back to Huntington's. Of course. Hell! This has to stop. I'm terrified, obviously. But I'm fed up with being terrified, which is winning out over the fear itself. Barbara would probably tell me it's a good sign. Life is a battle. Well, I'm fighting; therefore, I'm alive. At the magazine, I'm taking care of business with a certain efficiency. Nobody there suspects anything. Rumor has it, even, that I'm going to be promoted. Lots of money. My anxiety isn't paralyzing me.

I had lunch with an old friend. She knows everything. She was the one who honored me with that beautiful dedication in her latest book: "To my professor of courage." We talked, as usual, about some of our favorite targets: journalists, politicians, the powers that be. We laughed, as usual. Then she asked me about my blood test.

"When will you get the results?"

"I've only told Mary. Suppose I did give you the date and then, on that day, I don't call you. What would you do? Don't worry. I'll tell you the verdict when I get it. Fast."

"I'm not worried. You seem to be in great shape."

We have known each other for twenty years. I know she doesn't lie. But what good does it do me to look like I'm in great shape? I keep worrying. Naturally. This morning, coming off the metro, I stumbled a little. Like my brother. I panicked, naturally. So, to reassure myself, I ran down the twenty steps to my transfer. Perfect. Unbearable. It does not tell me anything at all.

What a weird test of nerves this whole business is! This incredible wait. The two possible outcomes could not be more opposite. What is it like—like waiting for the French baccalaureate results? Or the reaction of that editor, some years ago, who had me write twenty-five pages on the revolution in Romania, a place I'd never set foot in? No, no. In those cases, at least, you can always bounce back if you fail. No, this is more like the guy on trial for murder, waiting for the verdict. No, not even that. Because the murderer gets, at minimum, a life sentence. For him, the choice is either death or misery. For me, it's more like Russian roulette: a gun, two barrels, only one bullet, death or life. Or I'm a hostage. From my cage, I agonize over whether the noises in the corridor are bringing freedom or death. Light or darkness, death row or life row—which one will I get?

I slept like a baby. A peaceful dream, no tension, no fear. Why was I in New York, at the United Nations? Probably because I want to go back to the old days, when I was reporting on world affairs. Does it matter? What matters is that Huntington's was not in the picture then. I woke up with that realization—it was almost sensual, the perfume of absolute freedom. Is that the way it will be after D-Day? The day will be blessed, of course. Mary told me that would be the first day of the new season of *Friends* on TV. Thursday, 8 P.M. You cling to anything when you are afraid. And for Mary and me, *Friends* is the show from our happy days. When everyone was still at home, we would all watch together: the three kids, Mary, and me. Because . . . New York, because . . . the happiness of living, loving, and laughing. On April fourth, it won't be reruns anymore; the characters will have new adventures. It cannot be that their ideal, rosy world will be drowned in my damnation. I can already see my daughter laughing at Phoebe's blunders, Chandler's jokes, Monica's love-life plotting, and I'll be sitting there next to her, trying to digest the news from that morning—news of my end, of my death foretold. *Not* possible. Obscene. Unlivable.

Sometimes magic happens. I'm okay today. This must be my luck line, this metro line where they've started posting poems. Too bad this isn't D-Day, with me riding to my destiny. The poem in this subway car would be so "cool," as my daughter would say:

> *Even my shadow*
> *Is in perfect health*
> *First day of spring*

says the haiku by Issa, a Japanese poet who died in 1827.

My shadow is a few days early; spring is a week away. But I must be getting used to the wait, or convincing myself, unconsciously, that I have nothing to fear. Unless I'm feeling the weight—the very light weight—of my freedom to come. Overwhelmed until now, by the weight—the heavy weight—of the decision I had to make, to test or not to test, I'm like a prisoner freed from the jail of my obsession.

When we left home this morning, I told Mary, "In three weeks, at this hour..."

"The axe!" she said, laughing. The guillotine. It's a way to fend off bad omens. Or to express her confidence. And her fatalism. I laughed along. We are holding on.

I'm doing even better than that. In a restaurant today, I put someone in his place, an old big shot of the Mitterand world whom a colleague had introduced me to. He was known for his phony liberalism, his socialist views from a sumptuous apartment near the Eiffel Tower, and his multifarious unidentifiable sources of income. He took offense at my pro-American tendencies. What he liked was the antiglobalization militants gathered then for a big summit in Brazil.

"You don't look like you'd fit in too well in Pôrto Alegre," he said haughtily, from behind the smoke of his $60 Cuban cigar and his $400 lunch bill in this Champs Elysées restaurant.

"Whereas you look very Fidel Castro," I retorted. "And the neighborhood around here has an astounding resemblance to the Sierra Maestra, don't you think?"

I got up and left. "Well said," someone whispered from a nearby table. Really, though—with a revelation, my soon-to-be apocalypse, before me, I think I'm allowed a few little nasty pleasures, no?

I've had it with seeing symbols everywhere. Manon called me—
remember Manon? My first little breasts; the ones I was thinking
about as I listened to Souchon singing a few weeks ago: *"La vie ne
vaut rien, mais quand je tiens, dans mes mains, les deux petits seins
de mon amie, rien, rien, rien ne vaut la vie."* I haven't heard from
her in more than thirty years, before Huntington's. My mother was
beautiful, and my brother was handsome, and my sister... And
here she calls up, springing out of the past, telling me she's changed
husbands. She wants to see me. She wants me to help her budding-
journalist daughter find a job. She suggests April fourth. I almost
ask her if she would wear a big black cloak and carry a huge sickle.
I say no to April fourth. We'll see each other on April second. Shall
I dare? Why wouldn't I dare? Her call is just a coincidence.

Big musical show at the Stade de France, *A Celtic Night*. Performers have come from that whole world. Anyone who hasn't heard the infinite, inspiring, moving, wonderful lament of three hundred bagpipes playing "Amazing Grace" together doesn't know the immensity of our souls.

Heard a psychiatrist on a TV show. He said, "You should not be afraid of your fear." I'd like to see him in my shoes.

I'm sure Barbara lied to me: the doctors don't need a whole month to analyze blood, check the results, and check them again. What they're actually doing is giving you time to get used to the worst possible outcome. Today I think I could be doomed, and I'm facing up to that reality. I admit that I've set up my own little interior scheme, a secret code that enables "us," me and my potential tragic double, to coexist. My theory: the statistics show that I have a 50 percent chance of sickness; I'm aware of it; I am living with the idea; therefore I'm okay, because only healthy folks can be so lucid.

Not bad for a psychological cushion. Or crutch. A pathetic rationale, but it helps me get through. I even danced tonight. And laughed.

"You're looking serious tonight," Mary said, though, as we set out for a friend's fiftieth birthday party.

"Because things are serious," I replied. "Eighteen days to go..."

"Everything is fine so far," she said.

She is right. The air tastes good on the party barge. The logical Seine, as Fitzgerald described it, looks peaceful. The music is happy. There is friendship and beauty. A woman leads me into a sensual, oriental dance. She's an old friend. Her name is Barbara, just like my favorite doctor. Another sign, of course. A sign of what? A few steps away, Mary smiles at me. We slow-dance together. When we get home, we make love. We make love well. How could I be sick? A fifty-fifty chance. Eighteen days to go. So far, things are good. Like in the story of the guy who's falling from the thirty-fifth floor of a building: as he goes by the eighteenth floor, he yells, "So far, so good!"

I saw Jean-Paul Sartre's *No Exit* in a theater today. "Hell is other people," blah-blah-blah... He was totally wrong. Hell is oneself, all the shit in our heads. Hell is what keeps you from being totally clear about yourself, what you would want to know about yourself, all the control you would want to exercise over yourself. Hell is our powerlessness with ourselves. At one point though, Garcin, the hero, does say something right: "When there is no fear left, there is no hope left." Tonight I feel a lot of hope. I'm sleeping pretty well. Without Xanax. Still no Xanax, and I'm living normally. My brain must still be functioning. How far have they gotten with my blood?

Back to Edinburgh. For a rugby game between France and Scotland. Above all, for a pilgrimage. The last time I was there was forty-four years ago. The summer of '58. With my father, mother, brothers, and sisters, everybody alive and kicking, happy and healthy, in the old family Citroën that would overheat in the Highlands. Friends of friends had lent us their house. In the small garden, on the well-tended, thick grass, I would wrestle with my brothers. My little sister was wearing the kilt of some clan McSomething. My mother would send me shopping for groceries nearby. First she would have me repeat after her the English words she had written on a piece of paper. Then off I'd go, the proud little Frenchman. I would recite my lesson. The grocer would listen. And laugh. He did not understand a word, and always ended up taking my mother's list from me. I always brought home exactly what I was supposed to, and never told anyone that the man had read the note himself. My mother pretended that she believed me. She smiled. My brothers and sisters laughed themselves silly. Huntington was not a Scot.

Forty-four years later, I look for the house. I don't find it. Doesn't matter. France beats Scotland easily. After a victory against England. Maybe we'll beat Ireland, Italy, and Wales, too. A Grand Slam! Ain't life beautiful?

I was supposed to have lunch with my brother. I cancelled. Told him I was sick. It's only half a lie. I'm sick with the long wait, my fear of seeing myself in him, if ten days from now... I'm sure he didn't believe me. On the phone I heard a low moan. I almost explained everything to him. No. He would not understand, he could not understand that I want to be alone, that I need to be on my own. I've had enough of other people, telling young journalists how to write a lead, sympathizing with a poor soul who twisted her knee and can't come in to work, not speaking my mind to an obnoxious press attaché trying to sell his untalented bimbo singer. I am mean, unfair, with the woman from my previous magazine, who finds me ruthless and distant because I no longer pay enough attention to her. Today I'm obsessed with Diane Pretty, an Englishwoman who is in the news.

"It is a soul locked in an inert body," says the newspaper. "Sometimes her eyes fill with tears. Once in a while she shows a faint smile. But her life stops with her face, surrounded by peroxide blond hair, the last ultimate sign of self-pride. She is forty-three years old, paralyzed from the neck down, almost totally unable to speak.... In 1999 doctors diagnosed her with Lou Gehrig's disease, a degeneration of the nervous system. Fed through a tube, Diane Pretty's only prospect is the paralysis of her lungs and a slow stifling death. When she gathers up enough energy, she communicates by a small computer attached to one arm of her wheelchair. With her electronic voice, she has been repeating the same message for months, over and over, in one law court after another. She is demanding a dignified and painless death. She wants to die when she chooses, at home, surrounded by her loved ones." But the law bans her husband from helping her do what she cannot do by herself: end her life. So she went to Strasbourg, to plead her case before the European Court of Human Rights.

Why am I thinking about Diane Pretty? Because ten days from now, I, too, may have no other prospect but a slow and irreversible degeneration of my body and my soul, to which I must add the weight of the legacy to my children. I, unlike Diane Pretty, will be able to take my own life. How would I do it? I don't want to suffer. Xanax and Lagavulin together—would that be enough? A gunshot? Where would I find a gun? Anyway, that would be messy. Blood, bits of brain all over the place. Drowning? A plastic bag over my head? Too violent. There must be other ways, gentler ways, potions that allow you to go peacefully. Barbara must know them. I would need her help, or Mary's, just as Diane needs her husband's help. Would they give it? Certainly not. Because they would be accomplices to a crime, would have to stand trial. What crime? Why is this not one of the most elementary human rights, the right to a gentle release from unbearable physical and mental pain?

I'm not crazy, not yet. And I declare it calmly, rationally, certain of the rich happiness of my past life: I don't want a future as ruined as the striatum of a Huntington's victim. If I learn, in ten days, that I'm done for, I will have only one reasoned, reasonable, and rational objective left: to plan a good death before I'm eaten up from within by the locusts of my apocalypse. I will go find it in Holland or in Oregon. I hear that people there believe in a peaceful death. Why would that be offensive? Or even dramatic? Who could reproach me for it? It would not detract from my feelings for my loved ones. And who could accuse me of blasphemy against God or anyone else? I love life, and I would rather not have it come to that. But it would be a simple, serene statement that I've served my time, given what I had to give. For better or for worse. That would be my life plan, as the psychologist would say. Unless I could be useful for some kind of experiment likely to benefit research. A lab animal... That would be a great destiny. Otherwise, bye-bye... See you in another world.

It is dark. I can't sleep. I go over what I just wrote. I don't find it morbid or depressing. I am not really frightened anymore. Actually, I'm eager to reach a new stage in my life. I almost feel lucky. Huntington's compels me to reflect on what I care about, on who and what I am. Thus comes the miraculous feeling of some kind of inner peace. The closer I get to the verdict, the better armored my soul becomes. Whatever happens on April fourth, I'll have the same body, brain, organs, as today, when I'm writing these peaceful words. If this is lack of consciousness, let's hope it lasts! Full steam through the mud! I love that declaration of faith. There is a lot of mud. I still have a good supply of steam.

My father died today. Just like that, all of a sudden. As if a gigantic feeling of "I've had enough" suddenly overwhelmed him. Like a superb defiance, a great "fuck you" to the endless suffering of my brother, my sister, of all those people who cannot manage to live or to die. His life ended in a couple of seconds. The cleaning lady found him this morning, on the tile floor of his bathroom, lying on his back, mouth open, eyes half closed, his hand clenching his chest.

He had called me last night. He sounded so healthy, full of unusual energy for an eighty-seven-year-old. I told him so. Like all his Tuesdays, he had spent the afternoon with a small group of old friends. That always made him cheerful. Before that, he had had lunch with my brother. Instead of me, who had backed out. He had been happy to replace me. A few hours later, he was dead. Even before his head hit the ground, the doctor estimated. A heart attack, probably, as he was getting ready for bed. There he is, lying on the floor. Chance has it that I'm the first of his children to get there. I take his hand, already cold. I cry. And I wonder what it means, eight days before my D-Day. Probably nothing. What do two little vials I filled with my blood three weeks ago have to do with the sudden death of a man who happens to be my father? Surely though, there must be a message. Is God offering me a tragic preview of what I should expect a week from today? Or has He set up some kind of sacrificial rite, calling my father to Him, the better to spare me? A swap? Easter is in a few days, Holy Friday tomorrow. A Father, so they say, who sent his Son to die to save mankind. . . . In my case, it's my father whose already stiff body lies between the bathtub and the radiator of his little bathroom. A few drops of dried blood are on his neck. He must have hit the radiator when he fell. His face is peaceful. What a violent death, though! He had already taken the bedspread off his bed, but he had not lain down yet. His pajamas are ready on a chair next to the bed. He walks a few yards down the hallway to go and brush his teeth. And then . . . What do you think about when you are about to die and don't know it?

The undertakers are here. I choose his dressiest suit, the one with the little Legion of Honor ribbon on it, and a white shirt, a navy blue tie, dark but not gloomy. At last he is on his bed. His face is already gray. Everybody thinks it is best to take him to the funeral home. He will be better preserved there. My older sister and I go to choose a coffin. Phone calls, paperwork. Tears. Fears.

Only eight days left. I have to hang on.

I took my brother to the still-open coffin. He is so calm. He stands there, strangely still, before the corpse of this man he refused to see for such a long time. His wife had turned him against the man she considered an intermediary transmitter of Huntington's, a diabolical messenger from hell—even though he couldn't have known, poor dad—the source of her unhappiness. In this last year, though, the men had begun to see each other again. Mainly because it was convenient—they were neighbors, so my father could be useful. But at least my brother no longer hated him, I think. He stands there before him. He says nothing, of course. But for the first time in many months, he looks almost normal. Does he feel close to or distant from this lifeless body? Sad? Indifferent? Anyway, he does not seem—he no longer seems—angry.

The morticians have closed the coffin. Tomorrow is the funeral—in Brittany, beside my mother, close by the house with the immaculate wax-smelling floors, where one day, beneath a crucifix, she showed me her knitting and said: "See, even this I can't do anymore." We've sent lots of announcements. On those announcements, I wanted to use the word "death." I wanted to say that his children announced the "death" of their father. The officials said that "passing away" would be better. It would be less harsh, said the woman in charge. She must know better than anybody else about life, and death, sudden or slow. I let the expert have the last word on the matter.

We left for Brittany. At dinner that evening, one of my sons burst out crying. I bit my lips not to do the same. If I give up, if I let myself go . . . Not in front of them. I would have to explain everything to my children—tell them about the test, my insufferable waiting. Add fear to sorrow. It's too soon. I must hold on. Six more days.

A model funeral, a beautiful spring day. An old cousin remembered a fascinating thing: a few years before World War II, my father's younger brother had died of pneumonia in his early twenties. The cousin talked about him all day long, as of an overwhelming, ghastly shadow. And "I think we buried him on an Easter Saturday, too," he ended up saying.

We searched through old papers. It was true. The two brothers were buried on the same day, more than sixty years apart, the day before the day some people call "the Resurrection"! Am I overinterpreting? Oversymbolizing? Am I crazy? Am I ready for the born-again bunch? One of my friends, who curses priests morning, noon, and night, would never talk to me again if he knew I just wrote that. Still... My more recent friend, my guardian angel from Patmos, must be stroking his long, smooth beard. I'm sure he has a serene look on his face. I'll have to go and see him again.

My children sleep in the bedroom that my brother and I used, summers when we were boys. Some of the comic books of those times are still there. In the cracks between the slats of the wooden floor, I look for grains of sand that we shed as we were changing out of our bathing suits. The suits were woolen, scratchy, painful. Beautiful. Some posters are still stuck to the walls; we'd glued them on so that nobody could ever take them off. Ken Rosewall, Rod Laver... how we loved tennis. A horse running in the sunset... With my children, I look through old photo albums. The history of a family. Happy people. Healthy people, except for my mother toward the end. After that, no more pictures. I walk through the house. I sit on my parents' bed. The crucifix is still hanging. My mother's beautiful face is next to it, within its beautiful golden frame. The photo has a brownish tone, a Harcourt Studio kind of tint. I see her again with her piece of knitting. I hear her: "Even this I can't do anymore..." I open the big, beautiful Normandy closet with its doors that seem to come from a fifteenth-century church. White starched linen sheets are neatly folded. Suits and shirts hanging there. My father's clothes. My father's smell.

I don't want to come back to this house ever again.

I told that to my two older sisters and my other brother. Since we'll soon be talking about the inheritance, I'm not interested in the Brittany house. As for the rest, I ended up telling my sisters: "I don't know. I'm not making any plans. I took the test for Huntington's. In three days I'll know..."

I went back to work. Thank goodness, lots of meetings. And my lunch with Manon, "the two little breasts." Uneventful. She remembered my father. We talked about him. And about her daughter, who wants to go into journalism. Manon is still pretty. But I'm not in the mood for any funny business. I even started to panic. Quick, a Xanax. With a few more meetings, it takes me through to the evening. I'm drained. Exhausted. Angry. Impatient. The end is in sight. It's like when you run cross-country in winter. Your lungs are flaming. Your vision is blurred. But I'm about to make it to the finish line. In what condition?

What exhilaration and what anguish! Could there be a more intense questioning about life, a richer anguish over death? In ten hours I will know. I went through my day soothed by my comfortable routine. No Xanax. Which is a good sign, I kept telling myself, minute after minute. Which means nothing, I kept telling myself, minute after minute. Overcoming my anxiety today does not mean that my stupid micron-sized gene is not rotten; that in the extraordinary bio-genetic program that rules us all, it will not start to act up like a mad animal, set off cyclones in my soul that will make me insane.

I went home as I would on any normal day. I wondered if I should do that; I considered wandering through the city all night, looking for some new sensations that would bring me to the next morning in a daze, ready to hear anything in Barbara's office. Why would I do that? Powerlessness, absolute powerlessness, is my kingdom. I am in a situation that no new experience, knowledge, intuition, could change in the slightest. So wait. Half a bottle of whiskey, three cigars, soccer on TV. Liverpool is playing. "You'll never walk alone"—the fans sing the official club anthem like a choir. My father introduced me to the song. And to the game. On Sundays he would take his three boys to the park with the beautiful, round leather ball. He would team up with the oldest one against us little ones. The grass was a crisp green. Happy. We would never walk alone. Today the father is dead. My partner in soccer is done for. And I... "Eternity is long," Woody Allen says. "Especially towards the end." My eternity is coming to an end. It's long. A few more hours. Hold on. Sleep. I still have sixteen Xanax pills in my bag.

Tomorrow will I gulp them down? Or throw them away?

*Thursday, April 4: D-Day*

*Why did I come an hour early? How naive! As if hurrying could change anything about the verdict.*

*I barely slept. I had a dream, though, about Barbara. Barbara, of course! She was standing in the corner of her office. "Everything's okay," she said. Woke me up. What a nightmare! I got up. So did Mary. She hadn't slept much either. We didn't exchange a word. A few glances were enough. Anguished glances. I took a shower, got dressed. My best suit. Today deserves it. Dark suit. White-and-blue-striped shirt. Club tie, navy blue. Black shoes. I spent a few minutes polishing them. Keep the mind busy. Then I went. Alone. Mary will meet me there. I walked toward the metro. The fire station, the barber, the Algerian grocer, the flower shop— all those familiar landmarks suddenly become strange places, almost menacing. The markers of my anguish. The newspaper store. Buy a pile of them. Force myself to read them, as if nothing special was going on. Impossible. Each train stop becomes a station of my walk to Calvary, to the execution site. With a difference: me, shitty little terrified mortal, son of my Huntington's mother and my recently lightning-struck, recently buried father; me, little husband of Mary, little father of my children, little brother of my sick brother, big brother of my sick sister, little journalist in a state of perpetual rage—with the difference, a major one, that I still have some hope. That I do not yet know what awaits me.*

*Four metro stops until I change trains. Then thirteen to the hospital. People are going to work. All the faces look alike. I look like them, too. Yet how many extraordinary stories are behind those impassive features! Stories hiding there of love, separations, pleasure, misery, sickness, death. A street musician plays "Kalinka" on his accordion. I want to block my ears. Everything moves as slow as a snail. As a hearse.*

*The train stops at the Pasteur station. Pasteur, like the Institut Pasteur, where they discovered the HIV virus a few years ago. Through the window, on the platform, there is a quote celebrating science, research, and those who practice it. It is by François Jacob, a Nobel Prize winner from some years ago. "We no longer ask the gods about our future life or our children's lives. Now, we ask the genes." Bastard! What is the point of interrogating the genes? Of being able to interrogate them? And thus to learn your terrifying future? I remember an old conversation with a very bright geneticist, more than twenty years ago. He was talking about the miracles of predictive medicine. "What does that do for me?" I had asked. "What does it do for people at risk for Huntington's? How will it help for them to know when there is no cure for their fate? How are we going to go on?" In the fancy restaurant where we were having lunch, he had miserably started to talk about something else. What do scientists know of the suffering they dabble in? The hope and despair?*

*Ten more stops. The train alternates between tunnels and bright daylight. Day and night. On the platforms, posters, publicity, slogans.* ARE YOU READY TO HEAR THE TRUTH? *says one. It's an advertisement for a film with Andy Garcia, the story of a psychiatrist in whom a child confides about the death of a parent. Further along, at the last stop, another poster, for another film. It's called* Showtime. *What? Yes,* Showtime! *Time for the truth.*

. . .

*Waiting.*

*Mary has joined me, at last. Together we climbed the ramp to the Neu-rology/Genetics building of the hospital. We have not yet exchanged the least remark, except for mine to Mary: "How does it feel, going to the slaughterhouse?" She did not answer.*

*Barbara's office door is open. Barbara, the star of my* Showtime, *is not there. I can hear her voice, though. She is in her assistant nurse's office, where they drew my blood twenty-eight days ago. She walks out, sees me from the doorway. "Just a second," she says. "I'll be right with you. Take a seat."*

*We sit down in her office. Wait. Wait again. She would have told me in the hallway if I did not carry the gene. At least she would have winked. We have known each other for so long . . .*

*She comes in, shakes hands with both of us. I remember she told me she always said hello first, on Judgment Day. With a smile, whatever the result. She says hello. With a smile.*

*"Your name is Jean Baréma, born on June 14, 1949?" she asks.*

*"Yes."*

*"You do not carry the gene for Huntington's disease."*

*Mary bursts into sobs. So do I. Barbara's eyes are glistening. She tells me that the formal procedure is necessary, so that everyone at risk is treated equally as they approach the verdict. Suppose she told me right away in the hall and I mentioned that to other people awaiting results, if they later had to wait in her office for her to come tell them? They would conclude that they were doomed.*

*I am spared. Safe. And so are my children. Why? How did I deserve this, and not my brother or my sister? I cry. I tell Barbara that I want to take care of them, the sick ones. She tells me to first take care of myself, not to feel guilty. I ask her if I can give her a hug. I hug her. She smells good. Mary and I go to the café. We consider ordering champagne. Too early in the day. Coffee will do. I call my children, two or three close friends. As if this was a normal day, I go to work. There is a guy there whom I like and have known for a long time. He has gone through a few storms of his own in his life, and his weathered face often lights up with a serene smile. He finds me astonishingly joyful, and he tells me so. I recount the whole story, from start to finish. He grabs my hand, like an old rock-and-roller, thumb locked to thumb. We must look really stupid.*

    *I go home. Mary has prepared a glorious dinner. Champagne, caviar, lobster. With our daughter, we watch the new season opener of* Friends. *Happiness.*

    *Like before.*

    *Better than before?*

"What about your mourning?" the psychologist asks me.

A month has gone by since my father's death. I'm back at the hospital—the same one, by the same metro. The posters have changed. I no longer find hidden meanings in them. I saw Barbara in the hallway. She was talking to a patient, a real one. She gave me a smile and a friendly wave. Will she ever know what an impact she can have on people?

"My mourning? Okay," I say. "My father had a good death, insofar as there is such a thing."

"I wasn't talking about your father. I meant your other mourning. . . . Mourning the end of the danger."

She brings up an old conversation we'd had about "at risk" people who find out that they don't carry the gene and break down. Because they suddenly face a great void. "You remember what you told me when I asked about your life plan in case you were a carrier?"

I remember perfectly. I close my eyes. I repeat. "Commit suicide. Write. Leave my wife. Or love her, more and better, as she deserves. Tell the truth about politicians and journalists, and show business, and television. Become a serial killer."

"And if you weren't a carrier?"

"I said, the same. Except for serial killer, and suicide. That would be too dumb."

"That was the right answer. I know some people in your situation—they changed jobs, took lovers, wrecked their marriages, crashed straight into the wall in their overexcitement. You—what are you going to do?"

"I don't know. 'The wind is rising. You must try to live,' the poet said. For me, it's the opposite. The wind has died; what is going to help me live? Maybe I'll die of boredom. Or blow up.... But Huntington's, and the Patmos monk, have taught me to look at things differently."

I tell her about Péguy and his stone breakers at Chartres—the despairing *Untermensch,* the man serene with his fate, and the cathedral builder.

"It all depends on your angle, your take on life," I say. "Because eventually, we are all going to come apart. We'll all go through it. Yes, we've all got some Huntington's in us."